FOODS OF THE MAYA

A Taste of the Yucatan

FOODS OF THE MAYA

A Taste of the Yucatan

Nancy & Jeffrey Gerlach

The Crossing Press Freedom, CA 95019

Thanks for all your help...

Manuel Aguilar, Jane Jordan Browne, Robert Catts, Celia Cruz, Dave DeWitt, Dennis Hayes, Diana Kennedy, Josephina Lopez, Pat Padilla, Maria Perez, Erlinda Rios, Joe Romero, and Robert Spiegel. And a special thanks to Chuck Evans!

Cover Design by Sheryl Karas

Printed in the U.S.A.

Library of Congress Cataloging-in-Publication Data

Gerlach, Nancy.

Foods of the Maya: a taste of the Yucatan / by Nancy & Jeffrey Gerlach.

p. cm.

Includes bibliographical references and index.

ISBN 0-89594-675-0. — ISBN 0-89594-674-2 (pbk.)

1. Cookery, Maya. 2. Cookery—Mexico—Yucatan (State) 3. Yucatan (Mexico : State) — Description and travel. I. Gerlach, Jeffrey. II. Title.

TX716.Y83G47 1994

641.59'2974—dc20 94-995

CIP

In fond memory of Byrne and Lloyd.
Thanks for the wanderlust!

Contents

Introduction

Although we've been traveling south of the border for more than twenty-five years, we were introduced to the Yucatán only ten years ago. Our first trip, a snorkeling and diving vacation, was all it took for us to fall in love with this wonderful, magical place, and over the years we found ourselves returning as often as possible. There's a lot to like: the weather is just about perfect, complete with a rich, deep-blue sky filled with massive, majestic clouds; the forests are as vast and dense as they are mysterious; the Mayan ruins are both extraordinary and enigmatic; the palm-lined beaches are heart-wrenchingly beautiful; and the turquoise sea is warm, crystal-clear, and full of spectacular life. In addition, the cuisine is rich and varied and utterly delicious, and the people are some of the happiest and friendliest we've ever met.

Anyone who spends any time in the Yucatán will sense a pervasive happiness, a joy of life. The sound of laughter is never far off, and nearly everyone will return a smile for a "*Buenos dias*." We have never been in a place where so many people went out of their way to say hello, or to ask if we needed help.

Because it was physically isolated for so long by water on three sides, as well as by impenetrable forests on its southern border, the Yucatán was influenced more by Europe and the Caribbean than by Mexico. Thus, it has developed a cuisine that is distinct and separate from what is commonly called Mexican food.

Background Information

History

Despite some of the world's most impressive ruins, historians still cannot tell us what really happened to the Maya. Dates can be attached to sites, and it is possible to differentiate the various architectural styles, but nobody can answer the most important question, "Why did the Mayans walk away from these incredible cities?"

Civilization first appeared in the Yucatán about 2500 B.C., but no one knows whether the first settlers came originally from Mongolia and northern Russia or from southeastern Asia. By 300 B.C., much of the area was settled, and villages were established.

The next 600 years are referred to as the Classic period, which is acknowledged as the flowering of the Mayan civilization. During this time, religion became organized and dominant, and Mayan society became extremely complex and diverse, requiring specialized professions such as architects, scientists, mathematicians, and artists. This led to the creation of some of the world's most spectacular buildings and temples, a calendar so accurate that it continues to amaze scientists today, complex mathematical calculations that were the most advanced in the world at the time, and a vast array of artwork that is viewed with awe even thousands of years later.

Despite these intellectual achievements, however, these same people were extremely bloodthirsty. Blood sacrifices upon special blood-channeling altars were not uncommon, prisoners of war were routinely humiliated, degraded, tortured, and dismembered before being executed, victims (primarily children) were regularly thrown into the sacred wells (*cenotes*) to appease one or another god, and humans and animals were routinely sacrificed for the burial of leaders or rulers.

From 900 A.D. until the arrival of the Spanish in 1517, the light of civilization that had burned so brightly was slowly extinguished by nearly constant warfare. Throughout this period, most of the magnificent Mayan cities were abandoned, and by the time the Spaniards first landed, Mayan civilization had virtually ceased to exist. Despite being reduced to individual tribes, the Maya proved nearly impossible to conquer. Eventually, however, they were subdued more by deception, disease, and starvation than by physical force. After being defeated, they lived in virtual slavery for hundreds of years.

Following Mexican independence in 1812, the Yucatán suffered through over 100 years of armed rebellion and guerrilla warfare as the Maya again asserted their independence. Many simply did not want to be a part of Mexico, and for a number of years, various areas briefly claimed independence before being convinced, usually by overwhelming force, to rejoin the Republic. A peace treaty was finally signed in Quintana Roo in 1935; it was not until 1974, however, that Quintana Roo achieved Mexican statehood.

Archaeologists and historians have been trekking through the forests of the Yucatán ever since the publication of John Steven's intriguing travel books in the 1800s, searching for answers and generally finding questions instead. The ancient Maya remain mysterious, inhuman geniuses, builders of noble empires that were intellectually superior, yet they never developed the wheel, and they worshipped gods that required barbaric behavior and constant bloodletting.

Physical Characteristics

The Mexican Yucatán, which includes the states of Campeche, Quintana Roo, and Yucatán, holds approximately 1.75 million people and covers 43,500 square miles (about the same size as Ohio), with nearly one thousand miles of seashore. To the east lies the crystal-clear Caribbean Sea, while the northern and western shores are bordered by the murky Gulf of Mexico.

The Yucatán peninsula is a flat shelf of limestone covered by a thin layer of soil, sitting just above sea level. Vegetation along the arid northern coast, where the annual rainfall can be less than 10 inches, is thin. Further south, rainfalls get heavier and growth gets thicker and taller, producing dense forests, although they never turn into true, tropical rain forests as found further south in Guatemala.

There are no rivers in the northern portion of the Yucatán. Instead, water runs under the porous limestone, accessible in natural caverns, or huge natural wells called *cenotes*, or constructed wells. The *cenotes* and caverns were instrumental in the founding of many Mayan cities—aside from collected rainwater, these were the only sources of water for these cities.

The climate is tropical, but moderate. Winter temperatures range between 60 and 80 degrees Fahrenheit, summer temperatures from 70 to 95 degrees. Rarely does the temperature reach 100 degrees. The Yucatán has two seasons, wet and dry. May through September is the rainy season, October through April the dry season. Even in the rainy season, however, mornings are likely to be clear and sunny, and afternoon showers tend to be brief, usually occurring at the same time every day. The steamiest time of the year is the two-month period preceding the start of the wet season. (If you've been there then, you might argue that there really are three seasons: wet, dry, and sticky.)

Because of the warm and moderate climate, a wide variety of cash crops are grown throughout the Yucatán. In the north, the main crop is *henequen* (sisal), a shallow-rooted plant that thrives on the sparse soil. Warm weather fruits and vegetables of every sort grow easily and abundantly further south. Corn is the main crop of the peninsula and is grown almost exclusively for local consumption. Other major crops include avocados, papayas, mangos, many members of the citrus family, and a bewildering variety of bananas.

Due largely to their physical isolation, the Maya have managed to retain their identity, including their own language, dress, housing, cuisine, and physical characteristics. The Mayan dialects spoken today in rural areas are very similar to those spoken hundreds of years ago. We have found that it is relatively easy to find English speakers in most cities in the Yucatán; in rural areas, however, the question becomes "*Habla español*?" rather than "Do you speak English?"

Huipiles, the lovely, practical, embroidered white dresses worn throughout the Yucatán, have been worn by Mayan women for centuries. Throughout the countryside, virtually everyone lives in the thatch-roofed, windowless, single-roomed homes that have essentially remained unchanged for thousands of years. Images of these huts can be seen carved in stone at various Mayan ruins, such as on the north wing of the Nunnery at Uxmal.

All a visitor has to do is step off the plane in the Yucatán to see that modern-day Maya retain most of the physical characteristics of their ancestors. They remain small (averaging under 5 feet tall) with straight black hair, dark complexions, broad faces with high cheekbones, prominent noses, and muscular builds. We think that the Maya are a handsome, attractive people. We also found them to be some of the friendliest that we have ever met. We have frequently been approached by Mayans who apparently were curious about us, and just wanted to talk, or ask questions. We have never felt threatened by Mayans in our travels through the Yucatán.

Modern Maya are aware of the toys and tools of the twentieth century and occasionally will add a gadget or two to their life. For instance, we've seen satellite dishes beside thatch-roofed huts in extremely remote villages. But the Maya seem to prefer traditional ways. They live the way that they do by choice and are not overly impressed with mere things. And, judged by their apparent satisfaction, their quality of life seems to exceed that of most people whom we know.

The Yucatán remains, to this day, the least "Mexican" of any part of Mexico. For the most part, Yucatecans are a fun-loving, easygoing people, more than willing to live and let live, as long as nobody tries to interfere with their lives. Many have tried to dominate them and some have even succeeded for various periods, but in the long run the struggle has always proved too costly. The modern-day Mayans remain proudly independent and deeply rooted in their culture.

Mayan Ruins

We would urge every visitor to the Yucatán to see at least one of the major Mayan ruins. They are as fascinating as anything in Europe or Asia Minor. You should visit a ruin even if you can spend only an hour; you will still carry away rich memories that will not be easily forgotten.

Visiting a ruin without a bit of preparation, however, can be a nightmare so we'd like to pass on a few suggestions. The most important consideration is the sun: Don't forget sunscreen, especially if it's the middle of winter and you've shown up pasty white. Whereas it's relatively easy to judge when you've had enough sun while lying on the beach, it's much harder while you are absorbed in seeing the ruins.

Since you'll quickly get thirsty while exploring the ruins in tropical heat, and since there are usually no soft-drink machines around, always carry a bottle of water. We also like to carry several oranges, which can be welcome energy-boosters, especially at some of the larger sites. Since you're liable to be walking across roughly paved areas or climbing irregular staircases, wear sturdy closed shoes. If you're sensitive to insect bites, bring insect repellent.

Try to visit the more popular ruins, especially Chichén Itzá and Tulum, as early in the day as possible. Aside from avoiding the heat of the day, you can usually beat the crowds this way.

Since no admission fee is charged on Sunday, it is even more important to arrive at the ruins early on that day.

Every site has tour guides who will gladly show you around for a fee. We have found their nonstop chatter to be a combination of factual information and outright fantasy. They also have a planned tour which may not allow you time to climb to the top of an especially inviting pyramid.

Rather than hiring a guide, we generally rely on books, purchased beforehand or at the sites where they cost a bit more. Since so little is known about the ruins, anyone's fantasy is as good as anybody else's. If you travel with a video camcorder, be aware that a special permit is required to carry it into archaeological sites. You'll pay about $8.50 (in addition to the entry fee) for the privilege of taping each ruin. However, there is no special charge for using still cameras. Don't even think about taking anything from an archaeological site. There literally are piles of carved stone pieces lying around every site, including some very fine work. Mexico treats stealing from a site as a major crime. The police will lock you up, slap you with a high fine, and then take their time considering your release. They have absolutely no sense of humor about thefts of this sort.

Tulum, a walled city approximately 80 miles south of Cancún, is built on a cliff overlooking the Caribbean, and unquestionably has the most beautiful setting of any ancient Mayan city. However, most of the buildings have deteriorated badly. Because of the ruins' proximity to Cancún and Cozumel, as well as the unbelievably inviting beach within the city walls, Tulum is usually very crowded. There are an amazing number of large, well-stocked souvenir stores, plus a couple of restaurants that surround the parking lot and line the road into the site. We continue to visit Tulum mainly because of the great number of iguanas that we can always find on the city walls.

If you want a taste of what the early explorers experienced as they hacked their way through the forest searching for ruins, be sure to visit Coba. It is only an hour's drive from Tulum on a narrow but excellent road that runs through a thick, pavement-encroaching forest and a few tiny Mayan villages. Coba was at one time one of the largest of all Mayan cities, with an estimated six thousand to seven thousand structures, but so far only a small fraction has been uncovered. So the site is a bewildering collection of widely separated, unexcavated buildings, connected by dirt paths that wind through the jungle. This is one site where you must have a map and should consider hiring a guide.

If you stick to the main trails and don't go detouring after any of the colorful butterflies that visit the site in phenomenal numbers, you'll have a wonderful time. Although only a few structures have been excavated, several are more than worth the trip. One in particular, the great pyramid, stands 130 feet tall, nearly 12 stories; the view from the top justifies the taxing climb. Incredibly thick tropical forest surrounds the nearby lakes and stretches out to the horizon in every direction. Also visible are a few other structures that have been reclaimed from the jungle, as well as numerous vegetation-covered mounds or towers that appear to be more ruins waiting to be excavated.

On the other side of the peninsula, between Mérida and Campeche, is the only hilly country in the entire Yucatán. The Mayan ruins in this region are considered by many to be the most beautiful of all Mayan cities. The impressive three-story Palace at Sayil is a good example. Huge but graceful with succeeding offset structures creating wide terraces at each level, the building is richly ornamented with stone sculptures, carvings, masks, and rows of columns. Surrounded by tropical forest, this magnificent 200-foot-long palace brings to mind and indeed rivals some of the glorious buildings of ancient Greece.

Another richly decorated building is found just up the road at Kabah. Originally a very large city spanning both sides of the present road, the site is only partially restored and has only two major points of interest. The setting on the east side of the road is lovely, with a wide, undulating grassy area leading up to the restored buildings. The entire facade of the Palace of Masks is covered with masks of Chaac, the Mayan rain god. Over 250 masks are lined up in vertical rows along the 150-foot length of the building. Set out on the ground in front of the structure are the parts of possibly hundreds more masks, evidence of a continuing effort by archaeologists to piece together all the scattered parts of the puzzle that once was Kabah. The other major point of interest, a twenty-four foot high freestanding arch, lies across the road about one hundred yards down the path. This arch was once part of an ornate, monumental gateway into the city. Now standing alone in the center of a jungle clearing, the arch at one time marked the end of a 10-mile raised road of crushed stone leading to the crown jewel of the Puuc cities, Uxmal.

The first thing you see as you walk into Uxmal is the towering Pyramid of the Magician, unique because of its rounded sides. As with other Mayan pyramids, the climb to the top is challenging because of the steep angle, the irregular surfaces, and the narrow width of the treads. Although most people take the shortest, straight-up approach, we felt more secure zig-zagging up, which allowed us to place an entire foot on each step. Others fall back on a four-limbed climb, using hands as well as feet, which is certainly safe, if somewhat less than graceful. (We have to admit, however, that the four-legged climbers look less silly than those who come down on their butts, bouncing from step to step.) A frequent visitor to the site informed us that climbing the east set of steps, the ones that face the entrance, is easier than climbing the west set, which rise up in a dizzying 60-degree angle.

No matter how you get to the 120-foot top, the view is spectacular. The site, in the cleared areas below, is surrounded by lush green forest on all sides.

The Nunnery, directly west of the pyramid, is a group of four buildings enclosing a large central courtyard. The upper walls of all the buildings are decorated with intricately carved masks of Chaac, intertwined snakes, and intricate geometric patterns, together with carvings of humans, animals, and Mayan huts.

The other major structure at Uxmal, the Palace of the Governors, is considered by many to be the finest example of pre-Hispanic architecture in the Americas. The beauty of this building lies not only in its pleasing proportions and its intricate, delicate stonework, but also in its lofty position on top of three massive terraces. The complexity of the decorations on the upper walls is astounding, especially since they completely circle the 320-foot-long building; according to one source, over twenty thousand stones had to be cut to create this masterpiece.

For sheer grandeur and spectacle, Chichén Itzá is in a class by itself. Set upon acres of open, rolling grassy land in the midst of tropical forest, Chichén Itzá is staggering in scale. Since most of the structures are widely separated, they really don't look gigantic when viewed from afar. But when you get close, or climb to the top of a building, or walk to the far end of the site, the immensity suddenly hits home. The ancient Maya, despite their small size, were people with grand visions.

We found that a good map with brief descriptions, along with an active imagination, served us well as we wandered, slightly dazed, through the ruins. Virtually every structure is decorated with carvings or sculptured panels that are impossible to distinguish from a distance. But a close investigation will reveal magnificent panels depicting Maya in full ceremonial dress, animals such as jaguars and snakes, carved skulls, and enormous serpent heads.

Since the site is over two miles long from end to end and includes so much to see, exploring Chichén Itzá can be exhausting. To study everything you need at least two days, but even a short visit can give you a good feeling for this impressive site. A good place to start is from the top of the pyramid.

The nearby ball court is enormous, 257 feet long, 100 feet wide. It is difficult to imagine how it was physically possible to play the game given the heat and humidity, the heavily padded uniforms worn by the players, the 25-foot height of the stone rings through which the ball had to be thrown, and the duration of the games, reportedly hours long.

El Caracol, which lies across the highway, may be the only round building ever built by Maya. Close by are the massive Nunnery and attached Annex, both highly ornamented. Nearly touching the Nunnery at the northeast corner is a minuscule building absurdly named the Church, which consists mainly of an astonishing collection of carved masks, fretwork, and sculptures of the four creatures that held up the Mayan sky—the armadillo, the snail, the turtle, and the crab.

Travel Basics

Food Facts

Finding fresh food in the Yucatán is generally not difficult. Tiny villages often have only one "store"—typically in a villager's home—with a meager supply and selection of food. Larger villages and small towns usually have one home that serves as a butcher shop and another that sells canned goods and soft drinks. Fruits and vegetables may be scarce, since most families raise their own. Larger towns all have marketplaces. Small markets generally offer only fruits and vegetables, whereas the large ones sell anything from avocados to live animals. Most large towns also have stores selling canned goods, breads, baked goods, and soft drinks. Street merchants spread out a small box on a busy street corner, or wander through busy areas with neatly packed plastic bags, shouting out the price to every passerby. Peddlers with fruit and vegetable pushcarts also roam the streets, offering the ultimate in convenience: front-door service.

Modern supermarkets are beginning to appear in larger towns and cities. We find supermarkets a handy place to buy canned goods and search out new foods, like the jars of spicy pickled potatoes that we found on our last trip to Cancún. Fruits, vegetables, and herbs and spices are usually not as fresh in supermarkets as in open-air markets, and also usually more expensive.

Prepared food is just as easy to find. Larger villages typically have a stall or two at the market where food is prepared and sold. Most towns have a restaurant or two, along with a pastry or baked goods shop, in addition to the fast-food market stalls. In larger cities, restaurants abound, from tiny hole-in-the-wall operations with seating for four, to first-class establishments. In addition, numerous street vendors offer everything from tortas and tacos to ceviche. Many supermarkets offer a selection of reasonably priced, prepared foods, which we've found to be tasty and well worth the price.

Cold fruit-drink stands can be found all over the larger cities. Because the drinks are so delicious and refreshing, most do a brisk and continuous business, and we admit to being steady customers. Pastry shops offer spectacular selections of pastries, cakes, breads and rolls, and even flans. Ice cream is extremely popular, generally quite tasty, and available all over the cities. Even though we share meals, cut portion sizes, and throw dietary restrictions out the window, we know we will groan when we get home and step on a scale, but the food is so tasty, varied, and abundant that we are simply unable to resist.

Renting a Room

Hotel rooms can vary greatly, and we have found that a little legwork helps ensure a pleasant experience. The most important rule is to visit a room before renting it. Hotel personnel usually will simply hand over a room key if you ask. Once inside, lie down on the bed to make sure you can sleep on it. If the weather is warm, check to see that the fan or air conditioner works. You should also check to see where the room is located, and what kind of businesses are nearby. A room that overlooks a busy street can be noisy around dawn when all the trucks in town start their day, and a nearby disco can keep you awake till daybreak. If the hotel has a pool, check it out before putting on your bathing suit.

Many hotels provide bottled water, so you may not have to buy your own. If you are traveling by car, ask about parking. And, finally, make sure you can work the key in the front lock, and that the door to your room actually shuts and locks.

Airport Customs

If you haven't flown to Mexico in the past few years, you haven't experienced the traffic light system that is now being used by Mexican customs. Everyone entering Mexico is subject to being searched by customs agents. In years past, these inspections could cause hours of delay. In an effort to speed things up, red and green traffic lights have been installed at the customs area. As soon as you collect your luggage, you proceed to the light and push the button. If the green light comes on, the agents just wave you through; a red light means that they will ask you to open your bags for a cursory inspection. Most people get a green light. We generally wait, fussing with a suitcase strap, until someone gets a red light. Then we grab our bags and press the button, which is virtually always green.

Money Matters

On January 1, 1993, Mexico changed their monetary system by dropping three zeros, making the exchange rate 3 pesos (rather than 3,000) to the dollar. Prices are now marked with both the old and the new peso figures, and occasionally even in dollars. The best rates for changing money are usually at the banks. Many hotels will change money, but at lower rates. There are also independent money changers in the larger cities that offer lower exchange rates, but they can really save the day if you run short of pesos after banking hours or on weekends.

On the Road

If you plan to spend any time traveling through the Yucatán, we recommend going by car. The alternative is to go by bus. Unfortunately, buses tend to be somewhat unpredictable, of greatly differing vintages and states of repair, and inevitably unreliable just when you can least afford it. A car opens up innumerable options, especially when your time is limited.

Driving in the Yucatán is something of an adventure, with a slightly different set of rules than most of us are used to, but it's neither impossible nor suicidal. In general, we found the drivers in the Yucatán to be as good or as bad as drivers in the U.S.A.

To rent a car in the Yucatán, you must be at least twenty-five years old and have a valid driver's license, passport, and major credit card. Rates can vary depending on the season, the time of day, and your bargaining ability. We've learned that we can usually save some money by renting a car in town rather than at the airport. Even if insurance seems absurdly expensive, don't even consider renting a car without it.

It is important to know that gas stations are infrequent, and finding a gas station doesn't necessarily mean that it will be open, or that it has gas, or that the pumps work. So gas up your vehicle every time you get the chance. We use an excellent road map from International Travel Map Productions mainly because it shows which towns have gas stations.

Roads in the Yucatán are generally quite good, although in some areas there are more potholes than pavement. Most of the roads resemble small, narrow country roads in the United States. Since the only way to travel through certain swampy or densely forested parts of the Yucatán is by road, you are likely to encounter critters of all sorts. Many animals in rural areas may act as if they have never seen a car before and literally get too confused to move out of the way. The number of roadkills is astonishing. But the stream of lizards crossing the roads provides great comic relief as they stand up and zip across the road on their back legs; we named this frequent happening the Iguana 500. It also pays to expect the unexpected: one April, on the road from Tulum to Coba, we drove through swarms of butterflies so thick that we had to use our windshield wipers in order to see the road.

The greatest threat to backbone, vehicle, and mental stability is the speed bump. There are bumps before and after and often within every town, village, or collection of two or more huts in the Yucatán, so keep your eyes open and cross them at 1 mile an hour.

Travels Around the Yucatán

Mérida

Despite a population that exceeds five hundred thousand residents, Mérida is a comfortable city. Known as the White City because of all the white buildings, it caters to visitors.

It's hard for us to imagine not having a good time in Mérida. The variety and quality of food are amazing; the weather is warm and gentle; the architecture, which ranges from simple and primitive to ornate and downright gaudy, is unique; and the people are friendly and interesting.

Mérida has the reputation of being the cleanest city in Mexico. Spread out and sprawling rather than multistoried and crowded, the city retains much of its colonial heritage. Many of the older buildings in the city are distinctly European, with small second-story balconies and elaborate iron railings. They also have incredibly high ceilings to help keep the heat down, rooms of enormous size, carved wooden doors, and ornate door and window trim. Some of the most magnificent and best-preserved examples of these buildings can be found on Paseo Montejo, Mérida's Champs-Élysées. The immense buildings here contain consulates, banks, and hotels; in the past they were the mansions of the *henequen* magnates who vacationed abroad, sent their sons to the Sorbonne, and dressed in Paris fashions. Other turn-of-the-century mansions are scattered throughout the city. Many have been renovated to house museums, schools, or government offices; others are slowly disintegrating.

Finding your way around the city is easy once you know that north-south streets are odd-numbered and east-west streets are even. As a result, street numbers have little meaning, and, in fact, don't even exist for most buildings. Instead, reference is made to the cross streets and also to the tiles on the buildings at street corners. For example, on one building is a tile with a drawing of two bulls titled, "Los Dos Toros." In the 1800s, when there was a high rate of illiteracy, streets were known by the names of birds, animals, and other easily portrayed natural elements such as the wind or the moon. Painted signs or statues at street corners were used to identify each street. Even after the system of numbers was adopted in 1865, many corners retained their unique names.

Mérida offers an extensive choice of hotels, from expensive to dirt cheap. Our favorite is the Gran Hotel, which recently celebrated its hundredth anniversary.

Staying in the Gran Hotel is like traveling back in time to a period when style, grace, and ambience were as important as clean rooms and helpful service. It is situated less than a block from the central plaza and is moderately priced.

Mérida's huge central market is not to be missed; you can spend days exploring it and the surrounding area. Originally housed in one large building, it has spread into shops, stalls, and sidewalk enterprises all along the adjacent blocks. Vendors sell everything, from television sets to habanero chiles, from live birds to handmade clothing and tools. The market is also a great place to see crowds of Mayan women in their lively *huipiles*. It's a true Indian market of remarkable vitality.

For inexpensive local food, try the restaurant section upstairs in the market. Here you'll find a long line of kitchen stalls with tables and chairs in front and chalkboard menus. Staffed by aggressive and vocal women who fast-talk anyone they can lure into their places, these small restaurants provide authentic local dishes at bargain prices.

Mérida's one real fault is the traffic. Because the city streets are narrow, vehicles run right next to the sidewalks. If you sit at a sidewalk table for lunch you can be overcome by the noise and fumes. Mérida is an excellent place to shop for souvenirs. Hammocks and panama hats are available all over the town, in the stores, in the central market, and on the arms of an army of street vendors. Mérida offers a variety of free entertainment nearly every day of the year, well attended by residents and tourists alike. Every Sunday, many of the streets around the town square are closed to cars, and the entire town, it seems, turns out to enjoy the day. There are concerts and musical presentations, arts and crafts booths, and food vendors and balloon and toy salesmen everywhere. It's a joyous weekly celebration.

The serenade in Santa Lucia Park every Thursday night is also extremely popular. Tourists are definitely in the minority at this event, but they are warmly welcomed. The program includes band music, folk songs, and poetry readings, but the last item on the program, the dancing, is always the highlight of the evening. If you don't understand Spanish, you might find yourself growing restless during the folk songs and poetry, but do hang around for the dancing. The young dancers are practiced and enthusiastic, and the women are gorgeous in their heavily embroidered *huipiles* and flower-decked hats.

Progreso

Because the road between Mérida and Progreso is one of the busiest in the Yucatán, especially during the summer months, it is well maintained, and therefore a pleasure to drive. The 22-mile drive goes by fast, through the low, sparse brush of the arid northern Yucatán.

Just outside Progreso, the landscape changes from scrub to foul-smelling swamp. Despite the stench, the area is visually interesting, even surreal with the dead remains of trees sticking up out of the still water. The only sign of life are the various birds, including flamingos, which wade in the shallow water or perch on the dead wood.

Progreso is a busy little town with beautiful beaches and an astonishing pier. It is a summer retreat for Mexicans, especially Méridanos. As a result, many restaurants and other facilities are closed during the rest of the year. The north end of town, which is close to the beach, consists mostly of vacation homes, ranging from huge, beautiful mansions down to tiny, temporary-looking structures, all of them empty except during the summer months.

The beach is wide and beautiful, and it stretches on forever. Numerous palms line the Malecón (the oceanside drive), easily making this the prettiest part of town. The pier extends out father than you can see due to the shallow slope of the sea floor. The pier serves as one of the main ports of entry to the Yucatán, and large trucks continuously pick up cargos from docked ships. You can drive your car out on the pier for a look back at the town.

On our last visit, we decided to take the long way back to Mérida. Driving east on Highway 27 toward Chixulub Puerto and Telchac Puerto, we passed mile after mile of empty beach-front homes, interspersed occasionally with large hotels and timeshare complexes. Like Progreso, this area comes alive only during the summer months. Since most of the beach front is posted and fenced private property, access to the water is limited. But in the open, undeveloped areas a few dirt roads run to the beach. These are especially worth taking if you love a wide, deserted beach that stretches as far as you can see, with so many seashells you could collect them with a shovel.

In several hours of wandering up and down the beach that afternoon, we not only failed to see another person, but we never even saw a human footprint. With the temperature in the low eighties, a slight breeze blowing off the water, and the cloudless sky a brilliant blue, just a shade or two lighter than the sparkling blue ocean, that afternoon was one of the highlights of our trip.

Celestún

If you're staying in Mérida, get up with the sun for a visit to Flamingo Mexicano de Celestún Natural Park, which lies on the Gulf Coast directly west of Mérida. The best way to see the thousands of birds at the park is by boat, and the best time to take the boat trip is in the morning. (The afternoon sun can quickly burn off a couple of layers of skin if you're still out on the water, and fierce little thunderstorms tend to arrive after the midday siesta.)

Along the back roads between Mérida and Celestún you can see old haciendas surrounded by fields of *henequen*, practically the only commercial crop that will grow in the arid climate and sparse, rocky soil of the northwest Yucatán.

Access to the Natural Park is one kilometer east of Celestún, at the long bridge over the Celestún estuary. Although there are a few trails for walking or driving in the park, the only way to see the main attraction—the huge flocks of Greater Flamingos—is to hire a boat and travel up the estuary. The boats are visible at the main dock to the left as you cross the bridge. You're expected to bargain over the price, which you can cut considerably by joining with other visitors to form a larger party.

The estuary is up to a mile wide and 14 miles long. As we started down it, we could just barely see a faint pink line along the distant shoreline. The pink became more and more distinct until we found ourselves gaping at thousands and thousands of wading flamingos. When we got fairly close, our guide cut off the motor and quietly poled us in toward the birds, since flamingos frighten easily and will abandon their site if disturbed. Bring your binoculars and a telephoto lens for your camera.

Along with the flamingos are all sorts of other birds, from ducks and geese to cranes, storks, and egrets. We found the clamor of the birds unbelievable, and the spectacle stunning.

Ticul

Ticul is a busy little town sitting in the middle of the only hilly country in the Yucatán. About fifty miles from Mérida, the town is a perfect place to spend time while touring the nearby Puuc ruins. We spent a couple of days there on one of our trips, enjoying the friendly people and the slow and easy pace of the town. With a population of about twenty-five thousand, the town is big enough to have a few hotels and restaurants, yet small enough to avoid the problems of cities.

Throughout rural areas in the Yucatán, one of the major methods of transporting both people and goods is by *triciclo*, a large tricycle with a platform or seat between the two front wheels. Ticul's streets, especially in the market area and around the town square, are full of *triciclos*, each with a different load, many humorously overloaded.

Ticul is one of the main pottery centers in the Yucatán, as can be easily seen just driving around the town. From the pots and jars that are sitting out to dry in front of homes, it appears that every third or fourth person in the town is a potter. Unfortunately for tourists, most of the pottery is far too large and heavy to take home.

There is a factory called Arte Maya on the west side of town that does produce small pieces. This factory and school, run by artist Wilbert Gonzalez, produces museum-quality terra cotta reproductions of classic Mayan art. Pieces by Gonzalez, as well as some by his students, are for sale, and both the workmanship and the prices are awesome. The reproductions are so close to the real thing that Gonzalez once spent several months in a Mexico City jail, accused of stealing and trafficking in original Mayan art. The entire facility is definitely worth a visit.

We were mildly surprised to find two good restaurants in this tiny town. The first is the original Los Almendros, which specializes in Yucatecan food and now has branches in both Mérida and Cancún. Set in a huge old house, the restaurant serves good to excellent regional dishes.

The other restaurant is Los Delfines, which serves a varied and imaginative menu of Mexican food. Operating under a huge, wall-less thatch roof, the restaurant is a favorite of the locals. It is a little hard to find, since it is set back from the road behind a large metal gate.

One Sunday night, as we sat in Ticul's town square watching practically the entire population of the town stroll by, two roulette wheels were set up right in front of us. Neither of them would have made it in Vegas, but both did a steady business that evening. One of the wheels was homemade, with nails sticking up to divide the sections and a flexible piece of plastic that marked the winner. Instead of the numbers used on a regular roulette wheel, this wheel had crudely drawn flowers and birds; a bet could be placed, for instance, on one bird or two flowers. The payoff was two to one, and it appeared that the only bet allowed was 100 *centimes*, which is around 3¢. This wheel was run by a thin old gentleman who was chain-smoking so heavily that he could hardly find time to spin the wheel, pay off the winners, and clear the board. The second, more elaborate wheel was run by a young man with two assistants. Larger and finely balanced, this wheel obviously had not been made on the floor of someone's hut. Both the betting amount and the payoff were the same as the first wheel, but this wheel used not flowers or birds, but the symbols and numbers from a deck of cards, like the three of clubs and the jack of hearts. Both children and adults placed bets at the two wheels; in fact, anyone with 100 *centimes* was welcome.

Campeche

The once-walled city of Campeche, located on the Gulf Coast about 125 miles southwest of Mérida, is a very clean, friendly city with a swashbuckling, bloody past.

With its relaxed, lazy pace and small size, Campeche is a good town to explore on foot. We were impressed with the large shaded central plaza just to the south of the cathedral. The sidewalk along the waterfront is a pleasant place for a walk, especially at night, when a cool, sweet breeze blows. The town is comfortable to visit with its easygoing, cheerful pace.

We arrived in town just after noon, stomachs growling. Since we happened to park the car almost directly across from a nice-looking restaurant, we gave it a try. The restaurant turned out to be La Parroquia, a moderately priced, longtime favorite of local residents, which quickly became our favorite as well. Open twenty-four hours a day, it offers an extensive selection of Yucatecan and other Mexican dishes, including a wide selection of seafood, all served quickly and efficiently by a crew of friendly waiters.

We settled for a tasty, light brunch of *sopa de lima* and *papadzules* along with a couple of cold beers. When our meal arrived, we got our first look at the Campeche method of pouring a beer: instead of holding the glass in one hand and pouring with the other, the waiter sat the glass on the table and hooked the lip of the bottle over the rim of the glass. Tilting the glass slightly, he slowly poured the entire bottle of beer with a single hand. This unusual method is practical; it allows a waiter to pour with one hand while balancing a tray with the other.

We noticed the Hotel Colonial as we were leaving the restaurant and it turned out to be a treasure. Our second-floor room was comfortable, clean, and quiet. Although the furniture was from another era, it was spotless with its fresh coat of paint. The bathroom, obviously added on, was a marvel of space conservation: with a toilet, sink, and shower, it couldn't have taken up more than 15 square feet.

The old city at Campeche's center is roughly outlined by the remnants of forts and city walls that were erected three hundred years ago to protect the inhabitants from pirates. Because the plundered treasure of the New World was regularly routed through Campeche on its way to Spain, the city attracted ruthless pirates from around the world. Operating from a base 130 miles to the south, some of the most infamous pirates in history, including Henry Morgan, Peg Leg, and John Hawkins, regularly descended upon the city, pillaging, massacring, and burning on an epic scale for nearly one hundred and fifty years.

After losing untold millions of dollars worth of pilfered treasure, Spain finally agreed to help in the building of a massive stone wall around the city and out into the water, with immense sea gates through which ships had to pass before they could dock safely. After the wall was completed in the early 1700s, the city lived in relative peace.

Watch out for the tropical downpour here. One evening we heard raindrops start to fall on the plastic panels that shielded the open patio at the hotel. Within a minute or two the sound had grown to a roar. Now we understood why the curbs on the streets in town were so high: The water in the street outside the hotel was already overflowing the 20-inch curbs.

A tropical downpour is one of nature's most impressive shows. People caught in their cars were helpless. The water quickly rose up to the tops of the tires and caused most of the vehicles to stall. The few completely soaked pedestrians tried desperately to keep their footing in the raging water several inches deep on the sidewalk. After hammering the city for about thirty minutes, the rain quit, and ten minutes later most of the water had drained away, although we did have to take off our sandals to wade across a street or two on our way to dinner. By the next day nothing remained but a remarkably clean city and some heavy-duty humidity.

Xcalak

One of the most intriguing towns in the Yucatán is Xcalak, situated at the southernmost point of the Caribbean coast next to the channel that divides this portion of Mexico from Belize. According to our map, the only way to reach Xcalak is by a "seasonal road, or track." We couldn't help but wonder about this isolated little town with an unpronounceable name. Researching the town in a couple of guidebooks, we learned that it is a small fishing village in one of the most beautiful areas on the Caribbean coast and we decided to go. Making the trip, however, was a bit more complicated. In the first place, although Xcalak is only 30 miles from Chetumal as the pelican flies, it's about 125 miles by road. Xcalak is also nearly 120 miles from the closest gas station, and a long way from any market. So before we left civilization behind, we picked up a spare gas can as well as a supply of food and water.

We left Chetumal early one morning and headed north, unsure whether this little side trip was going to be an unpleasant survival drill or a trip to a tropical paradise. Since Highway 307 North is in excellent shape, we made good time up to Cafetal, the turnoff point. Highway 10, which runs east and south over to the Caribbean, is also in excellent condition, although considerably narrower than the main highway. Along the way, much of the land is swampy and filled with mangrove thickets.

When we reached the Caribbean the pavement ended, replaced by a 35-mile-long dirt road. Little more than a rough dirt track, the road is full of deep potholes, and we had to proceed at a crawl.

Because we knew that Xcalak offers limited accommodations, as we approached the town we stopped at every possible place looking for a mosquito-proof room. Had we brought hammocks (along with mosquito netting), it would have been easy. Right outside of town, we spotted the Villa Caracol, a brand-new, modern beach-front home with two guest rooms on the second floor. This comfortable retreat was built by Dwayne Campbell, a retired American, who lives on the ground floor with his wife. The large, comfortable guest rooms feature twenty-four-hour electricity, air conditioning, hot showers, and, best of all, drinkable water straight from the tap, courtesy of a reverse-osmosis water system.

Out in front, a long wooden cross-shaped pier runs out into the blue-green sea. Several huge hammocks are hung on the wide part of the pier, which is covered with a thatch roof, making it a wonderful place to relax and watch the waves. Because of the nearby swamps, there are many thirsty mosquitoes and no-see-ums (sand fleas). During the day, they are kept at bay by the breeze off the sea. At dusk, however, when the breeze stops, the bugs attack en masse, requiring industrial strength repellent.

After we checked in, there was just enough daylight to take a refreshing swim and spend a few minutes snorkeling. As the sun went down, we made our way into town, looking forward to some fresh seafood for dinner. Really just a village, Xcalak consists of three or four dirt streets that parallel the beach, lined with single-story, faded wooden houses. It didn't take long to find the town's two restaurants and a couple of little markets.

We ate at the Capitan Caribe restaurant, which features a sand floor, several long tables lined with chairs, and a high thatched roof complete with naked light bulbs. The restaurant has no written menu; the waiter simply told us what was available that day. We both cried "Stop!" after he mentioned fresh lobster. It came with rice, black beans, carrot salad, french fries, corn tortillas, and two big lobster tails. After paying our bill we walked out into the black of night. The only lights in sight burned weakly from the scattered houses. Since it happened to be a moonless night, the sky was luminous with the brilliant light of millions upon millions of stars. We returned to our guest house, applied repellent, and went out to the end of the long pier, where we spent a couple of glorious hours lying on our backs staring straight up into that awesome display of stars. After a sound night's sleep, we were up early enough to sit on the pier while the sun came up, and marvel at the tranquil water. That afternoon I went on two dives, and both were spectacular. The Belize Reef, which lines the coast, is the second longest barrier reef in the world, providing some of the finest diving to be found anywhere.

Cozumel and Playa del Carmen

Playa del Carmen, the mainland departure point for the island of Cozumel, was once a mellow little town catering mainly to Mexican tourists. It has now become a crowded gringo destination, complete with newly paved walkways, restaurants specializing in steaks and barbecued ribs, and new hotels under construction wherever you turn.

Nevertheless, it is still a lot less hectic and expensive than Cancún, and its beaches are as wide and white and beautiful as any on the east coast. There are still cheap hotels in Playa, as well as some very comfortable, expensive resorts, and many of the restaurants in town still serve reasonably priced local specialties, usually seafood. Despite the crowds, Playa del Carmen remains small and laid-back compared with Cancún.

Straight across the water lies the island of Cozumel. Thirty years ago, Cozumel was a quiet backwater, with nothing much happening and no particular place to go. Then Jacques Cousteau discovered that the island's west coast is bordered by more than twenty-five spectacular reefs, and scuba divers began an invasion that has not yet reached its peak. Diving and snorkeling are so popular on Cozumel that divers account for more than 50 percent of the tourists. Along with divers are the day-trippers from the cruise ships that anchor off the island every day. San Miguel, the island's only town, has become a shopper's and diner's paradise, with souvenir shops just slightly outnumbering restaurants and bars. However, the town has managed to remain friendly. After the shops close and on Sundays, everyone comes out to stroll, cassette sellers crank up the volume on their boom boxes and spread out their tapes, local musicians try their best to compete, and vendors appear with balloons, cotton candy, and popcorn.

Fresh seafood is available everywhere, cooked in a wide variety of styles, for a wide variety of prices. There are several elegant restaurants that will serve a sumptuous meal that will take a hefty bite out of your wallet. But there are also many, less pricey restaurants that offer excellent Yucatecan and Mexican food; we found several such places east of the plaza. Dress is casual at all the restaurants. Because of the great diving, there are dive shops everywhere, and the boat operators and dive masters are knowledgeable and experienced. Most dives tend to be drift dives, due to the strong underwater current that flows south between the island and the mainland. The water is remarkably clear and stays close to 75 degrees.

I had the best dive of my life on a trip to Cozumel a few years ago, when our dive group was visited by a family of dolphins. I will never forget that experience, during which I was so excited that I started shouting, even though I was 80 feet down with a regulator in my mouth. While the females and youngsters played off to one side, the large male dolphin, obviously curious about us, slowly circled our group. He swam within three feet of me, so close that I could see every nick and scratch on his body.

Cancún

Depending on whom you talk to, Cancún is either the best or the worst thing that ever happened to the Yucatán. Those lucky enough to have visited the area twenty-five years ago remember the quiet, gorgeous beach, with a simple room and several meals a day costing less than five dollars. Picked by computer as an ideal site for development, Cancún has become one of the largest and most successful beach resorts ever conceived. Cancún is Mexico's most popular vacation spot, and is almost surreal in its beauty and perfection. It offers warm, tropical weather, sparkling clear water, and a gorgeous blue sky. Many of the hotels that line the beach are so large and architecturally unique they have become tourist attractions themselves. As you might expect, night life in the city is diverse and nonstop. Every water sport imaginable, except perhaps surfing, is easily accessible. And, for the more adventurous, several of the finest Mayan ruins in existence are found within 125 miles of Cancún.

Unfortunately, there is no longer much of Mexico in Cancún. Tourists need not worry about a language barrier, because English is spoken everywhere, and dollars are usually more welcome than pesos. Prices are high. Traditional Yucatán dishes are almost never served in restaurants. To say that you have visited Mexico by going to Cancún is about the same as saying that you have visited the United States by going to Las Vegas.

Cancún is actually composed of two totally different cities. Cancún the playground, known as Cancún Island, is a 14-mile-long beach lined with magnificent hotels and other businesses dedicated to serving tourists. Cancún City, on the mainland, is also liberally sprinkled with tourist shops, hotels, and restaurants, but it is primarily a business center. This is where the Mexicans live, which means it is also the place to find more reasonable prices on everything. An excellent bus system makes travel between the two sections fast and easy.

One of our favorite pastimes on Cancún Island is hotel-hopping, which is most easily done from the beach, since it is entirely open to the public. Some of the hotel lobbies and central interiors are luxurious beyond belief. We've stood with open mouths gazing upon luxurious settings—acres of polished marble on floors and walls, enormous Roman columns stretching high to the ceiling; miniature tropical jungles, complete with parrots; a pyramidal atrium, with a skylight at its apex many stories overhead, and thickly growing vines and hanging plants draping themselves from floor to floor before falling free to the beautiful gardens below; and even a collection of ground-level pools fed by dazzling waterfalls, which break on an intermediate level, before spilling down to the main-floor pools.

Rooms in these hotels are equally lavish: they may include in-room safes, fully stocked bars, kitchens, remote-control TVs with cable, air conditioning and ceiling fans, hair dryers, irons and ironing boards, balconies or terraces with planters full of mature tropical plants, purified tap water, bathroom scales, robes, refrigerators, hot tubs, and, of course, spectacular views. If you can afford it, you can find it in Cancún!

Isla Mujeres

Eight miles east of Cancún, straight across a shallow, turquoise-colored bay, lies the island of Isla Mujeres. Visible from the Cancún shore, the island is a slender, eight-mile-long finger of tropical paradise composed of a small city with the same name, a good-sized naval base, several idyllic beaches, and a million motor scooters for rent. Fishing used to be the only industry on the island; today, tourists visit the island in staggering numbers during high season.

Isla Mujeres still provides visitors a glimpse of the real Mexico and the Yucatán. Life moves a bit slower on the island than in Cancún, streets are narrower, buildings are smaller and older, accommodations are more rustic, and prices are more reasonable.

Restaurants range from simple *palapas* on the beach to pricey establishments. Seafood is available everywhere, and although lobster is no longer inexpensive, delicious fresh fish and ceviche are reasonably priced. As in Cancún, there is little trace of any Yucatecan food. Aside from beach and water sports, there is really little to do on the island, which accounts for the lack of any real night life.

You have to get to Isla Mujeres by boat. There are express boats, private water taxis, large passenger ferryboats, and car ferries. The most convenient departure point for those staying on Cancún Island is the Playa Linda Pier. Slightly north of

Cancún City, easily accessible by bus, are Puerto Juarez (for passenger ferries) and Punta Sam (for automobile ferries). Numerous day-long tours are available on everything from sailboats to huge, multistoried barges. Most of these tours include stops for snorkeling, at least one meal, and all the beer or punch you can drink. We always visit the island whenever we go to Cancún, if for no other reason than to enjoy the crossing. The intense greens and blues of the water are some of the loveliest in the entire Caribbean. Our last trip from the island to Cancún was aboard the ferry on a gorgeous sunny day. While most of the passengers watched MTV down below in air-conditioned comfort, we rode with only six or seven others on the large open-air top deck, cooled by a gentle breeze and listening to great salsa music played over the ship's loudspeakers.

Valladolid

An easy 25 to 30 miles from Chichén Itzá, the city of Valladolid is a convenient and comfortable place to stay while visiting the ruins. Valladolid's hotels and restaurants are far less expensive than those at Chichén Itzá. If you can settle for clean, comfortable accommodations at bargain prices, together with a good selection of restaurants and a chance to rub elbows with the local people, you'll like Valladolid.

In the middle of a rich agricultural area, Valladolid is a slow-paced town where visitors have a good chance to witness everyday life in the Yucatán. Valladolid has been called the center of Yucatecan cuisine. The city's restaurants aren't very numerous, but every one offers authentic regional food, including the popular and delicious Valladolid sausage.

Across from the town square on the corner of Calles 39 and 40, the Municipal Bazaar features several mini-restaurants that are usually open only for lunch. They all operate out of tiny kitchens that line one wall of the market, with six or eight tables in front of each. We found the food to be tasty and authentic, and the prices good. Since all the menus looked the same, we picked one place at random and shared plates of *cochinita pibil* and *rellano negro*.

At the heart of town is the town square which gets crowded nights and Sundays. An ornate iron fence surrounds the entire square, and paved paths crisscross the square and circle the large central fountain. Throughout the park are numerous benches, including *confidenciales*, high-backed, S-shaped concrete benches that allow young lovers to sit close and hold intimate conversations without being able to touch.

Women in the region are renowned for producing the beautiful embroidered dresses called *huipiles*. Whereas many sell theirs to shops, others simply display theirs on the iron fence of the town square to sell to passersby. Prices there are the lowest we found anywhere in the Yucatán.

Because the city is situated inland, it does not receive the cooling sea breezes that keep the coastal cities comfortable, so we strongly recommend finding a hotel with a pool. After our last trek through Chichén, which took over five hours, we really felt the heat. A dip in our hotel pool, a couple of cold drinks, and an excellent dinner of *pollo pibil* was all it took to get us back on our feet.

Salsas and Seasonings

One thing you can always count on when eating in Mexico is that there will be a bowl of salsa or a bottle of hot sauce on the table with your meal. In our travels, we sometimes have to ask for silverware or napkins, but rarely ever do we have to ask for salsa. Salsa is essential to Mexican cuisine—eating a meal without it is like eating a bowl of cereal without milk.

The Yucatán is home to a number of unique salsas. Most of the region's fresh table salsas are made with the delicious but incendiary *habanero* chile, which is possibly the hottest chile in the world. Definitely the chile of choice in the region, the *habanero* is sold in enormous numbers in every market in the peninsula. Despite the risk of incineration, we urge chile lovers to try some of the tasty recipes that follow. Do use care: it's easy to get the roof of your mouth and your tongue burned; you may also get hooked on habaneros due to their wonderful flavor.

Another chile unique to the Yucatán is the *xcatic*, a hot, long, yellow variety. Used almost solely for salsas, it is virtually unknown outside the Yucatán. Red radishes, while not unique, are popular and a surprisingly good addition to salsa as we know it.

The most famous seasonings from the Yucatán are the *recados*, or seasoning pastes. Made from spices and herbs such as cinnamon, allspice, black pepper, oregano, cumin, black peppercorns, annatto seeds, and cloves, along with chiles and garlic, they were developed long before the arrival of the Spaniards. They are the basis for some of the most popular dishes in the Yucatán, including *pollo pibil* and *cochinita pibil*. Included in this chapter are the three main *recados*: *recado rojo* (red seasoning paste), *recado de bistec* (green seasoning paste), and *recado de chilmole* (black seasoning paste). *Recado rojo*, which uses red annatto seeds for color and flavor, is used for the mouth-watering *pibil* dishes and is widely loved throughout the Yucatán. All three *recados* are available ready-made in the markets, along with all sorts of culinary herbs and spices, and even banana leaves. The larger stalls display the colorful pastes mounded several feet high in large plastic or earthenware bowls. Locally made, these *recados* are sold by the kilo. *Recados* are also commercially produced and packaged; these packages are found on grocery store and supermarket shelves. Although packaged *recados* appear to sell well, we found them inferior to both homemade and locally produced versions.

Some of the following recipes call for ground annatto seed. Do try to purchase the seed in the ground form; the whole seed is about as easy to grind up as a steel ball bearing. Now we know what the ancient Maya used those three-foot-long mortars and two-handed pestles for, aside from grinding corn. If you can't find ground annatto, place the whole seeds in a spice or coffee grinder, grind them as fine as possible, then sift and grind the powder again.

Red Seasoning Paste

Recado Rojo

This, the most popular of all of the different *recados*, is very typical of the Yucatán. It is used to add both flavor and color to foods, and is most commonly used for *pibils*. The red color comes from the annatto seeds, which also add a unique flavor to this tasty paste. Available commercially as *achiote* paste, *Recado Rojo* is far better when prepared at home.

4 tablespoons ground annatto seeds
1 tablespoon dried oregano, Mexican preferred
10 whole black peppercorns
1/2 teaspoon salt
1 1-inch stick cinnamon
4 whole cloves
2 whole allspice berries
1/2 teaspoon cumin seeds
3 cloves garlic, chopped
3 tablespoons vinegar

Put the annatto, oregano, peppercorns, salt, cinnamon, cloves, allspice, and cumin in a spice or coffee grinder and process to a fine powder. Place all of the ingredients in a blender or food processor and purée to a thick paste, adding a little water if mixture is too thick.

Allow to sit for an hour or overnight to blend the flavors. The paste will keep for 3 to 4 weeks in the refrigerator.

Yield: 1/2 cup

Green Seasoning Paste for Beef Steak

Recado de Bistec

Although the title of this seasoning paste might lead one to believe that it is only used with beef, it is also used with other meats, as well as with fish, poultry, and even in some soups. This is the paste used to season *escabeche* dishes that are so popular in Valladolid.

1 2-inch stick cinnamon
2 teaspoons whole black peppercorns
2 teaspoons whole allspice berries
1/4 teaspoon whole cloves
1/8 teaspoon cumin seeds
1 tablespoon dried oregano, Mexican preferred
2 heads of garlic, roasted and peeled
1/2 teaspoon salt
2 tablespoons vinegar

Put the cinnamon, peppercorns, allspice, cloves, and cumin in a spice or coffee grinder and process to a fine powder. Place all of the ingredients in a blender or food processor and purée to a paste, adding more vinegar if necessary.

Allow the *recado* to sit for a couple of hours or overnight to blend the flavors. The paste will keep for 3 to 4 weeks in the refrigerator.

Yield: 1 cup

Black Seasoning Paste

Recado de Chilmole

This is the seasoning most often used with turkey and other meats such as meatballs. It can be delicious, despite its glossy appearance. Traditionally, it gets its black color from pouring alcohol over the chiles and letting them burn. This accounts for the somewhat "sooty" taste and gritty texture that some commercial pastes have. This version, although not completely authentic, is very tasty.

8 ancho chiles, stems and seeds removed
Hot water, to cover
10 whole allspice berries
1 tablespoon whole black peppercorns
1 tablespoon ground annatto
1 head of garlic, roasted and peeled
1 tablespoon dried oregano, Mexican preferred
1 teaspoon dried *epazote*
2 teaspoons salt

Toast the chiles until blackened, being careful that they don't burn. Soak in hot water for 15 minutes or until soft. Drain and reserve the water.

Put the allspice and peppercorns in a spice or coffee grinder and process to a fine powder. Place all of the ingredients in a blender or food processor and purée to a paste, adding some of the reserved chile water if necessary.

Allow the *recado* to sit for a couple of hours or overnight to blend the flavors. The paste will keep for 3 to 4 weeks in the refrigerator.

Yield: 1 cup

Chile-Vinegar Based Sauce

Adobo

Adobos were developed as a way to preserve meat in the days before refrigeration and are still very popular in Spanish-speaking countries. This sauce goes especially well with pork.

2 dried ancho chiles, toasted, stems and seeds removed
5 dried *guajillo* chiles, toasted, stems and seeds removed
Hot water, to cover
1/2 cup chopped onion
5 cloves garlic
2 tablespoons vegetable oil, divided
1 teaspoon dried oregano, Mexican preferred
1/2 teaspoon ground cumin
1/2 teaspoon ground cinnamon
1/4 teaspoon ground cloves
1/2 cup vinegar

Soak the chiles in hot water for 15 minutes or until soft; drain them.

Sauté the onion and garlic in one half of the oil until browned.

Place all of the ingredients in a blender or food processor and blend until smooth, adding more vinegar if necessary.

Sauté the purée in the remaining oil for 5 minutes. Allow to sit for a couple of hours or overnight to blend the flavors. This mixture will keep indefinitely in the refrigerator.

Yield: 1 1/2 cups

Ground Spice Mixture

Xak

The Yucatán is one of the few areas in Mexico where pre-blended spice mixtures are popular and therefore available in grocery stores. This is for use with chicken or any other poultry.

1 3-inch stick cinnamon
1 teaspoon whole cloves
1 teaspoon whole black peppercorns
2 teaspoons dried oregano, Mexican preferred
1/4 teaspoon cumin seed
1 teaspoon whole allspice berries

Place the ingredients in a spice grinder or blender and process to a fine powder. Sift if necessary. This dry mixture can be stored indefinitely if covered tightly in a jar.

Yield: 1/4 cup

Marinated Onions

Cebollas Encuridas

These pickled purple onions are a traditional accompaniment to a meal of chicken or pork *pibil* and are also popular with any number of other local dishes. They are found on virtually all tables throughout the Yucatán as a condiment, along with salsa and salt.

1 large purple onion, thinly sliced or coarsely chopped
Boiling water, to cover
10 whole black peppercorns
3 whole allspice berries
2 cloves garlic, minced
1 teaspoon dried oregano, Mexican preferred
1/2 cup water
1/4 cup white vinegar
1/4 teaspoon salt

Pour the boiling water over the onions, let sit for 1 minute, then drain. Discard the water.

Place all of the remaining ingredients in a pan with the onions and bring to a boil. Immediately turn off the heat and allow the onions to marinate for a couple of hours or days before serving. The onions will keep indefinitely in the refrigerator.

Yield: 1 to 1 1/2 cups

Note: This recipe requires advance preparation.

"Dog-Snout" Salsa

Xnipek

Pronounced roughly "schnee-peck," it is literally translated as dog's snout salsa. It supposedly gets its name because it's so hot that it can make your nose run. This fresh, fiery hot salsa or a close variation appears on most Yucatecan dining tables. Its flavor is best if eaten on the same day that it is prepared.

2 fresh *habanero* chiles, stem and seeds removed, chopped or substitute 2 fresh jalapeños or 3 serrano chiles
2 medium tomatoes, chopped
1 medium onion, either purple or white, chopped
1/3 cup bitter orange juice (see page 105) or substitute 1/3 cup lime juice, fresh preferred
3 tablespoons chopped fresh cilantro

Combine all of the ingredients except the cilantro and allow to sit for a couple of hours to blend the flavors. Add the cilantro before serving. This salsa will keep for two to three days, if the cilantro is added at the time you serve the salsa.

Yield: 2 cups

"Little-Pieces" Salsa

Salpicón

The first time we were served this salsa we were surprised by the use of radishes, which added not only flavor, but also an interesting texture to the salsa. For variety, add some diced tomatoes or avocados.

1 fresh *habanero* chile, stem and seeds removed, diced or substitute 2 fresh jalapeño or 3 serrano chiles
1 large red onion, diced
8 to 10 radishes, thickly sliced
3 tablespoons bitter orange juice (see page 105) or substitute 3 tablespoons lime juice, fresh preferred
3 tablespoons chopped fresh cilantro

Combine all of the ingredients except the cilantro, and allow to sit for an hour to blend the flavors. Toss with the cilantro and serve. This salsa should be used within two to three days.

Yield: 1/2 cup

Salsa La Parroquia

This simple yet very tasty salsa was always on the table of the La Parroquia restaurant in Campeche. It goes well with a variety of dishes and is delicious even with chips.

1 11-ounce can tomatillos, drained, coarsely chopped
3 tablespoons fresh lime juice
1 fresh *habanero* chile, stem and seeds removed, chopped or substitute 2 fresh jalapeño or 3 serrano chiles

Combine all of the ingredients and allow to sit for 2 hours to blend flavors. This sauce will keep for a couple of weeks in the refrigerator.

Yield: 1 cup

Green Salsa

Salsa Verde

This is an all-purpose green sauce that can be served over enchiladas or tamales, in *chilaquiles*, or even as a dip. The sauce tends to thicken as it sits, so you may have to thin it with a little water before serving.

1/2 pound fresh tomatillos or 1 11-ounce can tomatillos, drained
Water, to cover
1 medium onion, chopped
2 fresh jalapeño or 3 serrano chiles, stems and seeds removed, chopped
3 cloves of garlic, chopped
1/2 teaspoon sugar
2 tablespoons chopped fresh cilantro

If you are using fresh tomatillos, remove the husks and simmer in water to cover for 10 to 15 minutes or until they turn light green and are soft. Drain. Discard water.

Place the tomatillos, onion, chiles, garlic, and sugar in a blender or food processor and purée until smooth.

Stir in the cilantro and serve. This salsa will keep for a couple of weeks in the refrigerator if the cilantro is added before serving.

Yield: 2 cups

Avocado Sauce

Salsa de Aguacate

This rich sauce goes well with any poultry dish.

3 fresh or canned tomatillos
Water, to cover
2 avocados, peeled and pit removed
1 fresh *habanero* chile, stems and seeds removed, chopped or substitute 2 fresh jalapeño or 3 fresh serrano chiles
6 cloves garlic, chopped
1 small onion, chopped
Salt to taste

If you are using fresh tomatillos, remove the husks and simmer for 10 to 15 minutes in water to cover or until they turn light green and are soft. Drain. Discard water.

Place all of the ingredients in a blender or food processor and purée, adding a little water if needed to make the sauce smooth and creamy. This sauce doesn't keep.

Yield: 1 1/2 to 2 cups

Fresh Xcatic Salsa

Salsa Cruda Xcatic

Xcatic chiles are similar in appearance and taste to both banana and *güero* chiles. Since this chile is not found outside of the Yucatán, you can substitute one of the above chiles and still produce tasty results.

8 fresh *xcatic* chiles, roasted, stems and seeds removed or substitute fresh banana or *güero* chiles
1 medium onion, roasted and peeled
2 tablespoons bitter orange juice (see page 105) or substitute 2 tablespoons lime juice, fresh preferred
2 tablespoons vegetable oil
Salt to taste

Place all of the ingredients in a blender and purée until smooth. Allow the sauce to sit for a couple of hours to blend the flavors. This salsa will keep for 2 to 3 weeks in the refrigerator.

Yield: 1 cup

Yucatecan Tomato Sauce

Salsa de Jitomate Yucateca

This simple sauce, the basis for any number of Yucatecan dishes, is used in recipes throughout this book. Roasting the vegetables before using them is typical in the Yucatán and definitely imparts a distinctive flavor. Traditionally, a *molcajete* (stone mortar and pestle) is used to purée the vegetables, but a food processor or blender works just as well.

1 fresh *habanero* chile, roasted, stems and seeds removed, chopped or substitute 2 fresh jalapeño or 3 serrano chiles
4 medium tomatoes, roasted, peeled and chopped
1 small onion, roasted, peeled and chopped
1/4 teaspoon dried oregano, Mexican preferred
2 tablespoons vegetable oil
1/4 teaspoon salt

Place the chiles, tomatoes, chopped vegetables, and oregano in a blender or processor and purée until smooth.

Heat the oil and sauté the sauce for about 5 minutes. Salt to taste. The sauce will keep for a week in the refrigerator.

Yield: 2 cups

Variation
Salsa de Jitomate de Chipotle. Rehydrate 2 or 3 dried *chipotle* chiles in hot water for 15 or 20 minutes. Drain and remove the stems. Add the chiles when you are blending the ingredients of the tomato sauce and purée until smooth.

Appetizers

The most important food for the early Maya was corn, which is native to central Mexico. Research has determined that early inhabitants there were domesticating corn as early as 5000 B.C. It has also been estimated that corn accounted for up to 60% of the daily diet of the ancient Maya. They worshipped a Corn Goddess (among many others) and repeatedly included images of corn in their stone carvings and decorations.

Ironically, their adherence to a corn ritual cost the Maya dearly back in the mid-1800s. After serving as virtual slaves to foreign settlers for several hundred years, the Maya revolted in 1847 and by the following year had won back the entire peninsula, except for Mérida and Campeche. Both were ready to surrender when the Mayan forces simply quit fighting and returned to their homes because it was time to plant corn and corn was very important to them. The Maya were subsequently defeated, and nearly half the peninsula's Mayan population was killed in the process.

Corn remains the basic ingredient in the cuisine of today and is served in one form or another at virtually every meal. It is grown everywhere in the Yucatan, and although it no longer appears to be worshipped, it remains a fundamental element of life on the peninsula. Each morning, women in small villages can be seen making their daily trek to the village grinder, bringing in bowls and buckets of corn kernels, and then returning home with prepared *masa* that is primarily used to make up the day's supply of tortillas. It's also used to prepare a variety of tamales, which are extremely popular in the Yucatan.

In larger towns, *masa* vendors can be found throughout the local market. Other market stalls are home to tortilla mini-factories, where corn is turned into tortillas by effective but unsophisticated mechanical equipment. These delicious, hot tortillas are then sold by the kilo to lined-up consumers who carry off enough to last the day, generally a huge stack.

Antojitos are yet another way that great quantities of corn are consumed in the Yucatán. These "little whims" are essentially snacks that are usually eaten with the fingers, and are virtually all based on corn. Generally they consist of a filling or two enclosed by tortillas or *masa*, and take the form of small enchiladas, tamales, or tostadas. We think that *antojitos* are some of the tastiest foods in the Yucatan, and often make a meal of two or three different plates of these delicious snacks. The recipes that follow in this chapter include all our favorites.

Antojitos are also served as a free appetizer with drinks in larger restaurants. If your timing is right, it is entirely possible to eat a light lunch for the price of a couple of drinks. Of course, *antojitos* are also available on all restaurant menus, at snack shops, from numerous vendors at or around the local market, and even from street vendors. In our opinion, some of the tastiest of all were those we got from the local markets, and the prices just couldn't be beat. We usually just looked for the most crowded stall and shouldered our way in; after all, the locals would certainly know where the best food could be found.

Enchiladas Stuffed with Hard-Cooked Eggs

Papadzul

Very unique to the Yucatán, these enchiladas are traditionally served garnished with a green oil that is squeezed from toasted pumpkin seeds. (We have omitted that step from this recipe.) This is a very old recipe reputed to have been served by the Maya to the Spaniards when they arrived in the New World. The legend is possibly true since the name means "food of the lords."

2 large tomatoes, peeled and chopped
1 fresh *habanero* chile, stem and seeds removed or substitute 2 fresh jalapeño or 3 serrano chiles
2 fresh sprigs or 1 tablespoon dried *epazote*
2 cups chicken broth
1 small onion, chopped
2 tablespoons vegetable oil, divided
1 cup toasted pumpkin seeds, finely ground
8 corn tortillas
6 hard-cooked eggs, peeled and chopped

Combine the tomatoes, chiles, *epazote*, and broth in a pan. Bring to a boil and cook for 5 minutes. Remove and strain, saving both the tomatoes and the broth.

Sauté the onion in 1/2 of the oil until softened and add to the tomato mixture in a blender or food processor and purée until smooth. Sauté the sauce in the remaining oil for 5 minutes.

Heat the tomato broth and slowly stir in the seeds. Simmer until the mixture thickens and is the consistency of thick cream, stirring constantly. Be careful the sauce does not boil or it may curdle.

Dip the tortillas in the warm pumpkin seed sauce to coat and soften. Place some of the chopped eggs in the center, roll up, and place on a platter. Pour the remaining pumpkin seed sauce over the top, then the tomato sauce, and serve.

Yield: 4 servings

Note: If your tortillas are stiff, heat some vegetable oil until very hot and dip the tortillas in the oil for a couple of seconds. Drain.

Fried Filled Tortillas

Panuchos

These puffed tortillas, opened and stuffed with black beans, are one of the most popular snacks in the Mayan cuisine. Although the choice of toppings may vary, black beans are always used as the filling. These *panuchos* can be prepared and kept covered for a while before the final frying. The added flour is a trick that Yucatecan cooks use to make the *masa* puff in the hot oil.

Tortillas
2 cups *masa harina*
3 tablespoons all-purpose flour
1 1/4 cups warm water
12 corn tortillas
1 cup warm *Frijoles Negros* (page 87)
Vegetable oil for frying

Topping
2 cups topping: *Cochinita Pibil* (page 53) or substitute cooked shredded chicken
***Cebollas Encuridas* (page 23) or substitute raw chopped onions**
Sliced avocados
Chopped fresh cilantro
Grated *queso fresco* or substitute Monterey Jack cheese

Combine the *masa* and flour. Slowly add the water, mix well, and knead for 5 minutes. Divide the *masa* into 12 balls and press into small tortillas. Cook the tortillas on a hot griddle. They should puff up as they cook, but if they don't, press lightly on the tortilla and it should puff. (If using prepared tortillas, turn them every few seconds until they puff up.) Remove and cool slightly.

Make a pocket in the tortilla by making an incision in the top (the part that puffed up) about 1/4 inch from the edge and 1/4 of the way around the tortilla. Blow into the tortilla to let the steam out and to keep it from sticking together.

Place 1 tablespoon of the beans in the pocket and flatten the top to seal. Keep the *panuchos* from drying out by covering with a slightly damp cloth or plastic wrap.

Pour the oil to a depth of 1 to 2 inches and heat to 350 to 375 degrees. Fry the *panuchos*, a couple at a time, until they are just crisp around the edges. Drain.

To assemble, top the *panuchos* with the shredded meat, onions, avocado slices, cilantro and cheese. Serve with a hot sauce or salsa on the side.

Yield: 12 servings

Note: If you can't get the tortillas to puff up enough to make pockets, layer two tortillas with the beans in between. Although not authentic, they will still be tasty.

Chaya Tamales

Dzotobichay

Chaya, a leafy green vegetable, is used in these tamales as a wrapper, or, more commonly, it is added to the *masa*. Since *chaya* is impossible to find outside of Mexico, swiss chard or spinach can be substituted and more conventional tamale wrappers used.

2 cups *masa harina*
1/2 teaspoon salt
3/4 cup chicken broth
1/3 cup shortening
1 pound fresh *chaya*, swiss chard, or spinach, cooked and drained, chopped
Banana leaves or other tamale wrapper
8 ounces toasted pumpkin seeds, finely ground
6 hard-cooked eggs, peeled and chopped
2 cups *Salsa de Jitomate Yucateca* (page 26)
String

Mix the *masa* and salt. Slowly add the broth until the mixture holds together. Whip or beat the shortening until fluffy. Blend in the *masa* and the chopped *chaya* or chard.

Press about 3 to 4 tablespoons or 1/4 cup *masa* into a 1/3-inch-thick rectangle on an 8- x 10-inch banana leaf or other wrapper, leaving a border on all sides of the *masa*. Sprinkle 1 tablespoon of the ground seeds lengthwise down the center of the *masa*. Next spread 2 tablespoons of the egg followed with 2 to 3 tablespoons salsa. Fold the leaf over the *masa* as tightly as possible and fold under the ends. Tie the tamale around the center with string.

Stand tamales upright on steamer rack over boiling water. Cover and steam until the *masa* pulls away from the wrapper, about 1 1/2 hours, adding water to steamer as necessary.

Serve with extra sauce on the side.

Yield: 4 to 5 servings

Note: These tamales can be prepared in advance and refrigerated before being steamed.

Fried Masa Boats

Picadillo Garnachas

Appetizers similar to these are served all over Mexico and are called *sopes* or *chaulpas*. Basically, they are tartlets of fried *masa* filled with black bean paste and topped with a variety of foods. Although a *picadillo* topping is called for in this recipe, any type of topping can be used. For example, in the Campeche market we ate simple *garnachas* filled with black beans and topped with shredded chicken and avocados.

Picadillo

1/2 pound ground beef
2 tablespoons vegetable oil
1/4 cup chopped onion
1 fresh *habanero* chile, stems and seeds removed, minced or substitute 2 fresh jalapeño or 3 serrano chiles
2 medium tomatoes, roasted, peeled, and chopped
2 teaspoons chopped fresh cilantro
1 tablespoon golden raisins, soaked in water to plump, drained
1 tablespoon slivered blanched almonds

Garnachas

1 cup *masa harina*
1/8 teaspoon salt
3/4 cup water
Vegetable oil for frying

Filling

1 cup warm *Frijoles Negros* (see page 87)
1/2 cup warm *Salsa de Jitomate Yucateca* (see page 26)
3 tablespoons finely grated *queso seco* or substitute Romano cheese

Sauté the beef in the oil until almost done. Add the onion and chile and continue to sauté until the onions are soft. Stir in the tomatoes and cilantro and simmer until the mixture is fairly dry. Add the raisins and almonds.

Mix the *masa* and salt together. Add the water, a little at a time, to form a soft dough. Divide the *masa* into 12 equal pieces, roll into balls, and then flatten each ball. Using both thumbs, make a well in the center and press out the sides to form a small basket or boat about 1/4 inch thick and 3/4 inch high on the sides.

Pour the oil to a depth of 1 to 2 inches and heat to 350 to 375 degrees. Fry the *garnachas*, hollow side down first, until they are slightly crisp on the outside. Drain hollow side down.

Cover the bottom of each with some of the beans and then a layer of the *picadillo*. Top with the sauce, garnish with the cheese and serve.

Yield: 6 servings

Little Black Ones

Salbutes Negritos

Sometimes called *sambutes*, these little puffed corn tortillas get their name because of the black bean paste that has been added to the *masa*. These are probably the most common fast food found in the Yucatán.

Tortillas

2 cups *masa harina*
4 tablespoons all-purpose flour
1 teaspoon salt
4 tablespoons *Frijoles Negros* (page 87), thinned
1/2 cup water
Vegetable oil for frying

Topping

2 cups cooked shredded chicken, or 2 cups *Cochinita Pibil* (page 53)
***Cebollas Encuridas* (page 23) or substitute chopped raw onions**
Shredded cabbage
3 fresh *xcatic* chiles, stems and seeds removed, chopped or substitute fresh banana or *güero* chiles
1 medium tomato, thinly sliced

Mix the *masa*, flour, and salt together. Add the beans and enough water to make a stiff dough. Let the dough sit for five minutes.

Pinch off pieces of dough to make 1-inch balls. Flatten into tortillas about 4 inches in diameter and cook on a hot, ungreased griddle until lightly done. Then fry the tortillas in hot oil until crisp. Drain.

Top the *negritos* with the chicken, onions, cabbage, chiles, and tomato.

Yield: 12 servings

Pompano Tamales

Tamales de Pámpano

Cooks in the state of Yucatán are fond of flavoring *masa* when making tamales. This recipe uses *achiote* paste to add both flavor and color to the *masa*.

Filling

3 cloves of garlic, chopped
1/4 teaspoon ground black pepper
1/2 teaspoon ground cumin
3 tablespoons *Recado Rojo*, divided (page 21) or substitute *achiote* paste
1/2 cup bitter orange juice, divided (see page 105) or substitute 1/2 cup lime juice, fresh preferred
1 1/2 to 2 pounds of pompano or other firm whitefish, cubed
1 small onion, chopped
2 tablespoons vegetable oil
2 tablespoons chopped fresh cilantro
1 small tomato, chopped

Tamales

4 cups *masa harina*
1 teaspoon salt
2 cups chicken broth
2/3 cup shortening
Banana leaves or other tamale wrapper
String

Place the garlic, pepper, cumin, 1 tablespoon of the *Recado Rojo* or *achiote* paste, and 1/4 cup bitter orange juice in a blender or food processor and blend. Pour the mixture over the fish and marinate for 2 to 3 hours.

Sauté the fish, along with the marinade and onion, in the oil until the fish is almost done, about 5 minutes. Add the cilantro, tomato, and rest of the orange juice and continue to cook until filling is fairly dry.

Mix the *masa* and salt together. Slowly add the broth until the mixture holds together. Whip or beat the shortening, along with the remaining *achiote* paste, until fluffy. Blend the *masa* and the shortening.

Press about 3 to 4 tablespoons or 1/4 cup *masa* into a 1/3-inch-thick rectangle on an 8- x 10-inch leaf (main rib removed), leaving a border on all sides of the *masa*. Divide the filling among the tamales and place down the center of the *masa*. Fold the leaf over the *masa* as tightly as possible and fold under the ends. Tie the tamale around the center with string or the reserved rib from the banana leaves.

Stand tamales upright on steamer rack over boiling water. Cover and steam until the *masa* pulls away from the wrapper, about 1 1/2 hours, adding water to steamer as necessary.

Yield: 8 to 10 servings

Note: This recipe requires advance preparation.

Vegetable Tamales

Tamalitos de Verduras

Tamalitos are small tamales. They can be served as an appetizer and also as a side dish with a meal in place of a vegetable.

Filling

2 dried ancho chiles, roasted, peeled, stems and seeds removed, chopped
2 cups cooked, finely diced carrots
2 cups cooked, finely diced potatoes
1 cup cooked peas
6 fresh tomatillos, cooked and chopped or substitute canned tomatillos, rinsed well
1/2 small onion, minced
1 teaspoon cumin seeds, crushed

Tamales

4 cups *masa harina*
1 teaspoon salt
2 cups chicken broth
2/3 cup shortening
Banana leaves or other tamale wrapper
***Salsa Verde* (page 25)**

Combine all of the ingredients for the filling.

Mix the *masa* and salt together. Slowly add the broth until the mixture holds together. Whip or beat the shortening until fluffy.

Add the *masa* mixture to the shortening and continue to beat.

Press about 1/4 cup *masa* into a 1/3-inch-thick rectangle on an 8- x 10-inch leaf, leaving a border on all sides of the *masa*. Divide the filling among the tamales and place down the center of the *masa*. Fold the leaf as tightly as possible and tie the tamale around the center with string or the reserved rib from the banana leaves.

Stand the tamales upright on a steamer rack over boiling water. Cover and steam until the *masa* pulls away from the wrapper, about 1 1/2 hours, adding water to steamer as necessary.

Serve the *tamalitos* with the *Salsa Verde*.

Yield: 24 servings

Enchiladas from the State of Quintana Roo

Enchiladas al Estilo de Quintana Roo

The combination of different chiles for the sauce is common throughout Mexico, but the use of nuts or seeds to thicken the sauce is very typical of Mayan and Yucatecan cooking.

Sauce

4 dried ancho chiles, stems and seeds removed, toasted
2 dried *pasilla* chiles, stems and seeds removed, toasted
Hot water, to cover
1/4 cup toasted almonds
2 tablespoons roasted peanuts
1 tablespoon vegetable oil
2 cups chicken broth

Vegetable oil for frying
12 corn tortillas

Filling

2 cups cooked shredded chicken
1 small onion, chopped
1/2 cup grated *queso asadero* or substitute Monterey Jack cheese

Soak the chiles in hot water for 15 minutes to soften. Drain. Reserve the water.

Place the chiles and the nuts in a blender and purée until smooth, adding just enough of the chile water to make a medium thick sauce. Sauté the mixture in the oil for 5 minutes. Stir in the broth, bring to a boil, reduce the heat, and simmer for 15 to 20 minutes or until the sauce thickens.

Pour the oil to a depth of 1/2 inch, heat, and fry the tortillas for a couple of seconds to soften. Drain.

Dip a tortilla in the sauce and place in a baking pan or casserole. Place some of the chicken and onion in the center and roll, making sure the loose end is on the bottom. Repeat until all the tortillas are filled. Top with more sauce.

Place the enchiladas in a 350 degree oven for 15 minutes or until hot.

Garnish with the cheese and serve.

Yield: 8 to 12 enchiladas or 4 servings

Shrimp Enchiladas

Tacos Rellenos de Camarón

Seafood enchiladas are a pleasant change from the more common cheese or chicken varieties. Many cooked seafoods including any shredded whitefish, chopped scallops, or even squid and octopus can be used.

Sauce

5 dried ancho chiles, stems and seeds removed
Hot water, to cover
2 tomatoes, roasted and peeled
1 large onion, chopped
1/2 teaspoon ground cinnamon
2 tablespoons vegetable oil

Vegetable oil for frying
6 corn tortillas

Filling

1 pound shrimp, cooked and peeled
2 tomatoes, chopped
1 small onion, chopped
1/4 cup chopped fresh cilantro

Garnishes

***Cebollas Encuridas* (page 23) or substitute chopped raw onions**
Shredded cabbage
Chopped radishes

Soak the chiles in hot water for 15 minutes to soften. Drain. Discard water.

Place the chiles, tomatoes, onion, and cinnamon in a blender or food processor and purée until smooth. Sauté the sauce in the oil for 10 minutes.

Combine all the ingredients for the filling.

Pour the oil to the depth of 1/2 inch, heat, and fry the tortillas for a couple of seconds to soften. Drain.

Dip a tortilla in the sauce and place in a baking pan or casserole. Place some of the filling in the center of the tortilla and roll, making sure the loose end is on the bottom. Repeat until all the tortillas are filled. Top with more sauce.

Place the enchiladas in a 350 degree oven for 15 minutes or until hot.

Garnish with the marinated onions, cabbage, and radishes before serving.

Yield: 6 servings

Mexican Tortilla Turnovers

Quesadillas Mexicanas

Simple and easy to prepare, this Mexican version of a toasted cheese sandwich is great cut into wedges and served with a cold beer.

6 corn tortillas
4 ounces grated *queso fresco* cheese or substitute Monterey Jack cheese
1 small onion, minced
2 teaspoons chopped fresh *epazote* or substitute 1 teaspoon dried
1 small avocado, sliced
Vegetable oil

Place 1/6 of the cheese, onion, and *epazote* on one half of the tortilla. Arrange the avocado on top and fold the tortilla over.

Toast the tortilla on a lightly oiled griddle until the cheese melts. Cut into in wedges and serve.

Yield: 6 servings

Pumpkin Seed Dip

Sikil-Pak

This recipe is most likely based on a very early Mayan sauce. It can be served as a dip with crisp fried tortillas or as a table sauce and accompaniment to grilled foods. It will keep for a couple of days in the refrigerator.

2 medium tomatoes, roasted and peeled
1 fresh *habanero* chile, roasted, peeled, stem and seeds removed, minced or substitute 2 fresh jalapeño or 3 serrano chiles
2 cups toasted pumpkin seeds, finely ground
2 tablespoons chopped fresh cilantro
2 tablespoons chopped onions
Salt to taste

Cover tomatoes with water, bring to a boil, reduce the heat and simmer for 15 minutes. Drain.

Place the tomatoes and chiles in a blender or food processor and purée until smooth.

Stir the tomatoes into the ground seeds until the sauce is the consistency of mayonnaise. If the sauce is too thick, thin with water.

Add the cilantro, onions and salt to taste, and let sit for an hour to blend the flavors. Serve at room temperature.

Yield: 1 to 1 1/2 cups

Stuffed Cheese

Queso Relleno

This may seem like an odd Mexican dish except for the fact that the state of Quintana Roo is a free port and imported cheese from the Netherlands is inexpensive. You don't have to use the whole round of cheese; a couple of servings can be prepared in a wedge. Serve with spoons so people can scoop out the inside and sop up the sauce with corn tortillas.

1 4-pound round of Edam cheese
1 pound lean ground pork
1 onion, chopped
2 fresh jalapeño chiles, stems and seeds removed, chopped
3 cloves garlic, minced
1 teaspoon dried oregano, Mexican preferred
1 large tomato, peeled and puréed in a blender
1/4 cup chopped green olives
1/4 cup seedless black raisins
3 tablespoons capers
4 hard-cooked egg whites, chopped
1 tablespoon red wine vinegar
1/2 teaspoon freshly ground black peppercorns
1/4 teaspoon ground cloves
Vegetable oil
Cheesecloth

Sauce
2 tablespoons butter or margarine
2 tablespoons all-purpose flour
1 large tomato, peeled and chopped
Pinch of saffron
2 cups chicken broth

Peel the wax off the cheese and cut a 1/2 inch slice off the top to serve as a lid. Hollow out the inside of the cheese, leaving a 1/2-inch shell and save the cheese for the sauce.

Sauté the pork, onion, chiles, garlic, and oregano until the meat is done. Drain off any excess fat. Add the tomato purée, olives, raisins, capers, eggs, vinegar, pepper and cloves to the meat.

Simmer for 5 minutes.

Spoon the mixture into the cheese. Place the lid on the cheese, oil the outside well, wrap with the cheesecloth, and tie securely.

Place the cheese on a rack in a steamer and steam over medium heat for about 15 minutes or until the cheese softens. Be careful that the cheese does not touch the water or it will become mushy.

To make the sauce: Melt the butter and sauté the flour for a couple of minutes. Combine the tomato, saffron, and the broth. Stir into the flour-butter mixture and simmer until the gravy thickens slightly. Add a cup of the reserved crumbled cheese.

Remove the cloth from the cheese and place the cheese on a serving platter. Remove the lid, pour the sauce over the cheese and serve.

Yield: 8 to 10 servings

Note: Any remaining cheese can be wrapped, refrigerated and used for cooking.

Soups and Salads

Although both soups and salads can be found on menus in the Yucatán, quite often they are not what we generally consider a soup or salad. Historically, the Maya cooked much of their food in the form of a soup. These were not, however, simple soups. They were instead loaded with many different vegetables, herbs and spices, meat, poultry, or fish, or any combination of the three, along with fruits and even seeds or grains. We would call these dishes thick, hearty soups or stews, and to this day this is what often passes for soup in the Yucatán.

Ordering a bowl of soup in Mexico is always fun because in many cases what you get may not be what you were expecting. We remember a meal in Ticul when we thought we were getting some kind of rice soup, only to find that we had ordered a rice dish that included peas and bananas! We had forgotten that menus sometimes list two kinds of *sopas* (soups): *sopas aguadas*, or wet soups, and *sopas secas*, which are dry soups. Recipes in this chapter include only wet soups.

The most famous soup from the Yucatán is *Sopa de Lima*, or lime soup. Made from limes, chicken, and a variety of herbs, spices, and seasonings, this tasty soup even includes tortilla strips. Mérida is well known for this dish, and having eaten the soup in many different places in the Yucatán, we would have to agree that Mérida restaurants serve the best. They consistently serve a soup with a body and a strong lime flavor, unlike the thin, watery soup that we occasionally encounter in other areas. When it is properly prepared, the soup is superb, and much of the credit must go to the small, tart Mexican limes. We love these strongly flavored, mouth-puckering fruits, and never return home without several kilos of them. (Although most citrus is restricted, it is okay to bring these limes back to the U.S.; just be sure to declare them.)

Salads are also quite different in the Yucatán. In the first place, there is no official salad course in the cuisine. Tourist restaurants have learned that many visitors prefer them and will serve familiar tossed salads, but this is definitely not *comida tipica* (typical food). The preferred way of eating raw fruits and vegetables is in combination with other foods. Most fresh salsas, for instance, are simply chopped fresh vegetables which are used as a condiment along with a meal. Guacamole can be considered a salad, but it too is generally used with other food, rather than eaten as an individual course.

Finally, we have eaten a number of cooked dishes that we would classify as a salad, even though they go against conventional wisdom, which says that salads consist of raw vegetables or fruits. For instance, we include a recipe for Mexican Salad made with *poblano* chiles and onions that are lightly sautéed, then added to avocados and hard cooked eggs, and tossed with vinegar. Sounds like a salad to us, and incidentally, it tastes great. Another recipe in this chapter includes jicama and oranges and could easily be called either a salsa or a salad. We enjoy it as both by simply varying the size of the ingredients. To use as a salsa, we chop everything finely; as a salad, we chop the ingredients into larger pieces.

Regardless of their classification, the following recipes include a lot of very tasty food. We have come to enjoy the fact that when we experiment with new recipes, we are not only eating new foods or new combinations of old foods, but we're also eating in an entirely new style, without regard to our own traditional standards. This is just part of the fun of experiencing a new culture.

Lime Soup

Sopa de Lima

This delicate soup is very popular throughout the Yucatán. The Mexican limes that are used in the Yucatán differ from the Persian limes that are common in the United States in that they are smaller, darker green, and more tart than sweet. Although they are preferred, any lime can be substituted.

3 corn tortillas, cut in strips
Vegetable oil for frying
2 chicken breasts
1 small onion, chopped
2 cloves garlic, chopped
6 whole black peppercorns
1 2-inch stick cinnamon
8 whole allspice berries
1 tablespoon chopped fresh oregano, Mexican preferred
4 cups chicken broth
1 tomato, peeled and chopped
2 tablespoons lime juice
1 fresh green New Mexican chile, roasted, peeled, stem removed, chopped
4 lime slices for garnish
Chopped fresh cilantro for garnish

Deep fry the tortilla strips in a 360 degree oil until crisp. Remove and drain.

Place the chicken, onion, garlic, peppercorns, cinnamon, allspice, oregano, and broth in a pot. Bring to a boil and remove any foam that comes to the top. Reduce the heat and simmer, covered, for 30 minutes. Allow the chicken to cool in the stock.

Remove the chicken and take the bones out. Using two forks, shred the meat. Strain the broth and add enough water to make 1 quart of liquid.

Reheat the broth with the tomato, lime juice, and chile. Add the chicken and simmer until the chicken is hot.

Place some of the tortilla strips in the bottom of a soup bowl, add the soup, garnish with a lime slice and cilantro and serve.

Yield: 4 servings

Vegetable Soup with Cheese

Caldo de Vegetal con Queso

Chaya, a leafy green vegetable, is popular throughout the Yucatán. According to Mexican cooking authority Diana Kennedy, "*chaya* has a sweetish flavor when cut fresh." As a substitute, she uses "swiss chard (not the red one) as it comes nearest in texture to *chaya*."

1 medium onion, chopped
2 cloves garlic, minced
2 fresh jalapeño chiles, stems and seeds removed, minced
2 tablespoons butter or margarine
1/4 pound ham, diced (optional)
4 medium tomatoes, peeled and chopped
1 pound *chaya*, rinsed and chopped or substitute swiss chard or spinach
1 cup cooked garbanzo beans or substitute small navy beans
1/4 teaspoon ground cumin
4 to 5 cups water
2 potatoes, cooked, peeled and diced
1 cup grated *queso anejo* or substitute romano cheese

Sauté the onion, garlic, and chiles in the butter until soft. Add the ham and tomatoes and sauté for an additional 5 minutes.

Combine the onion mixture, *chaya*, beans, cumin and water. Bring to a boil, reduce the heat and simmer for 30 minutes. Add the potatoes and simmer for an additional 15 minutes or until the potatoes start to break down.

Add the cheese just before serving.

Yield: 6 servings

Avocado Soup

Caldo Xochitl

There are several different avocado soups that are served in the Yucatán. One is served warm with rice, and the other, this recipe, is served cold and is very refreshing on a hot Yucatecan day.

4 cups chicken broth
1 fresh serrano chile, stem and seeds removed, chopped
2 large tomatoes, peeled
2 avocados, Haas variety preferred
2 tablespoons lime juice
Salt to taste
Lemon or lime slices for garnish

Simmer the broth, chile, and tomatoes for 20 minutes. Place in a blender or food processor along with the avocados and lime juice and purée until smooth. Season with salt.

Keep refrigerated until just before serving. Garnish with a citrus slice and serve.

Yield: 4 to 6 servings

Los Almendros Venison Soup

Sopa de Venado Los Almendros

A small red deer is indigenous to the Yucatán and venison is popular there. This recipe is a variation of a soup served at the restaurant Los Almendros.

2 tablespoons *Recado Rojo* (page 21) or substitute *achiote* paste
1/2 cup bitter orange juice, divided (see page 105) or substitute 1/2 cup lime juice, fresh preferred
2 pounds of venison, chopped, along with the bones or substitute beef
1 head of garlic, roasted, peeled and chopped
2 teaspoons dried oregano, Mexican preferred
1 teaspoon of freshly ground black pepper
1 teaspoon chopped fresh cilantro
3/4 teaspoon dried *epazote,* divided
1 fresh *habanero* chile, stem and seeds removed, chopped or substitute 2 fresh jalapeño or 3 serrano chiles
Water, to cover
1 to 2 tablespoons vegetable oil
2 medium tomatoes, peeled and chopped
1 small purple onion, chopped
10 radishes, chopped
2 fresh *xcatic* chiles, stems and seeds removed, sliced into rings or substitute *güero* or banana chiles
Chopped fresh cilantro for garnish

Thin the *Recado Rojo* or *achiote* paste with 1/4 cup of the orange juice.

Place the meat along with any bones in a large pot. Add the remaining *achiote* paste, garlic, oregano, pepper, cilantro, 1/2 teaspoon *epazote*, and habanero chiles. Cover with water, bring to a boil, reduce the heat, cover and simmer until the meat is done and starts to fall away from the bones.

Remove the meat, discard the bones, and, using two forks, shred the meat. (Reserve the remaining broth.) Fry the meat in the oil along with the tomato, onion, and the remaining *epazote*. While the meat is frying, pour the remaining orange juice over the mixture.

Place some of the meat mixture in the bottom of a soup bowl, add the broth. Garnish with the radish, chile rings, and chopped fresh cilantro.

Yield: 4 to 6 servings

Bean Soup with Pork

Sopa de Frijoles Puerco

This hearty soup could also be served as a stew. Just add hot tortillas, *Xol-Chon* (page 50), and you have a whole meal.

Soup

2 cups black beans
1 pound boneless pork, cut into 1 1/2-inch cubes
1 large onion, finely chopped
4 cloves garlic, chopped
2 tablespoons vegetable oil
1 fresh *habanero* chile, stem and seeds removed, chopped or substitute 2 fresh jalapeño or 3 serrano chiles
1 teaspoon dried *epazote*
3 tablespoons chopped fresh cilantro

Garnish

1 large onion, chopped
12 radishes, chopped
1/3 cup chopped fresh cilantro
1 fresh *habanero* chile, stem and seeds removed, chopped or substitute 2 fresh jalapeño or 3 serrano chiles
Juice of 2 limes

Cover the beans with water and soak overnight. Remove the beans, measure the water, and add enough water to make 6 cups.

Sauté the pork along with the onions and garlic in the oil until the onions are soft.

Add the pork to the beans along with the remaining soup ingredients and simmer until the meat and beans are both tender, about 1 1/2 hours.

Combine the garnish ingredients.

Remove the pork and beans with a slotted spoon and place them in the center of a warmed platter and arrange the garnish on the plate. Serve the bean liquid in soup bowls and let people add the meat, beans, and garnish to their bowls.

Yield: 6 servings

Note: This recipe requires advance preparation.

Fish Soup

Sopa de Pescado

Traditionally this soup or stew was prepared using the fins of a sea turtle or *caguama*. But since they are in danger of becoming extinct, firm white fish has been substituted.

1 pound of firm whitefish, such as pompano, snapper, flounder, or bass
Water, to cover
2 onions, chopped, divided
1 head of garlic, roasted, peeled and minced, divided
1 tablespoon dried oregano, Mexican preferred
2 tablespoons vegetable oil
2 carrots, peeled and chopped
1 potato, peeled and chopped
1/2 cup fresh peas
2 cups finely shredded cabbage
2 tomatoes, roasted, peeled and chopped
2 fresh jalapeño chiles, stems and seeds removed, chopped
2 bay leaves
1/2 teaspoon freshly ground black pepper
2 tablespoons lime juice
Chopped fresh cilantro for garnish

Cover the fish with water and add 1/2 of the onion, 1/2 of the garlic, and oregano. Simmer until the fish is just cooked. Remove the fish, let cool, remove the skin and cut in small chunks. Strain the broth and reserve.

Sauté the remaining onion in the oil until soft. Add the remaining garlic, carrots, potato, peas, cabbage, tomato, and the chiles and sauté for an additional 5 minutes.

Add enough water to the reserved fish broth to make 6 cups. Add the vegetable mixture to the broth along with the bay leaves and pepper. Simmer for 15 to 20 minutes or until the vegetables are just done. Add the fish and simmer for an additional 5 minutes.

Remove the bay leaves, stir in the lime juice, garnish with the cilantro and serve.

Yield: 6 to 8 servings

Beef Stew

Carne en Caldillo

Chile dulce is a multilobed, bright green, sweet chile that resembles a very large *habanero*, except that it has no heat. Since it is virtually unknown outside of the Yucatán, substitute a bell pepper. This stew is unusual in that it uses native *yerba buena*, or spearmint, as a flavoring.

2 pounds lean beef, cut in 1 1/2 inch cubes
Water, to cover
3 tomatoes, peeled and chopped
2 fresh *chile dulce*, stems and seeds removed, chopped or substitute 1/2 cup chopped bell pepper
3 fresh *xcatic* chile, stems and seeds removed, chopped or substitute fresh *güero* or banana chiles
1 large onion, chopped
2 cloves garlic, minced
2 tablespoons vegetable oil
2 teaspoons dried cilantro
1 teaspoon dried oregano, Mexican preferred
1 tablespoon dried *yerba buena* or substitute mint
1 teaspoon ground allspice
4 tablespoons of *Recado Rojo* (page 21) or substitute *achiote* paste
1/2 cup water
1 zucchini squash, chopped
1 chayote squash, peeled and chopped
6 radishes, diced
3 tablespoons of chopped fresh cilantro
1/2 cup bitter orange juice (page 105) or substitute 1/2 cup lime juice, fresh preferred

Cover the meat with water and simmer until very tender, about 30 to 45 minutes.

Sauté the tomatoes, chiles, onion, and garlic in the oil until soft. Add to the meat along with the dried cilantro, oregano, *yerba buena*, and allspice.

Mix the *Recado Rojo* or *achiote* paste with a half a cup of water and stir into the broth. Add the two squashes and continue to simmer until they are done.

Combine the radish, fresh cilantro, and orange juice. Serve this as an accompaniment to the *caldillo*.

Yield: 8 servings

Avocado Salad

Guacamole

This classic is popular all over Mexico. Serve as a salad and garnish with fried tortilla chips.

2 avocados, diced
1 tomato, finely chopped
1 jalapeño chile, stem and seeds removed, minced
1 tablespoon fresh lime juice

Combine all of the ingredients and mix well. Place the pit in the salad, cover with plastic and press it onto the surface of the guacamole to retard browning. Allow to sit for an hour to blend the flavors.

Yield: 1 1/2 cups

Cactus Salad

Ensalada de Nopalitos

Nopales are the leaves or pads of the prickly pear cactus. Where they are available fresh, street vendors peel and cut them in small strips and wrap them in cellophane.

2 to 3 cups *nopales*, cut in thin strips or 1 16-ounce jar of *nopalitos*, drained and rinsed
2 fresh serrano chiles, roasted, peeled, stems removed, chopped
1 small purple onion, sliced into thin rings
1 large tomato, diced
1/4 cup sliced black olives
2 teaspoons chopped fresh cilantro
1 tablespoon olive oil
1 1/2 tablespoons red wine vinegar
2 ounces freshly grated *queso asadero* or substitute Monterey Jack cheese

If using fresh *nopales*, cook in salted water until soft, drain and rinse. Combine the cactus, chiles, onion, tomato, and olives. Toss with the cilantro, oil, and vinegar. Garnish with the cheese and serve.

Yield: 6 servings

Mexican Salad

Ensalada Mexicana

This salad is unusual because the chiles and onion are cooked, rather than raw.

3 fresh *poblano* chiles, roasted, peeled, stems and seeds removed, cut in strips
1 small onion, sliced into thin rings
2 tablespoons vegetable or olive oil
2 avocados, sliced
2 to 3 tablespoons white vinegar
2 hard-cooked eggs, peeled and sliced

Sauté the chiles and the onion in the oil until softened but still crisp. Drain and cool.

Toss with the avocados and vinegar. Season with salt.

Place on a platter, garnish with the eggs, and serve.

Yield: 4 to 6 servings

Jicama-Orange Salad

Xol-Chon (Kek)

It makes a nice accompaniment to grilled meats and can also be served as a chilled fruit dessert.

2 oranges, peeled and sectioned
1 small jicama, peeled and diced
1/4 cup bitter orange juice (page 105) or substitute 1/4 cup lime juice, fresh preferred
2 teaspoons ground chile de árbol or substitute ground red New Mexican chile
2 tablespoons chopped fresh cilantro

Chop the oranges in roughly the same size pieces as the jicama and combine the two.

Mix the orange juice and chile powder. Pour over the jicama mixture and toss well.

Allow the salad to sit for an hour to blend the flavors.

Toss with the cilantro and serve.

Yield: 2 cups

Meats

Although by no means scarce, meat dishes are not as popular in the Yucatán as in other parts of Mexico. Certainly the never-ending supply of seafood is part of the reason, as well as the great number of game birds, including turkeys, pheasants, ducks, and geese that are found in the Yucatán. Despite the introduction of beef, lamb, and goat, most current meat dishes have their roots in pre-Hispanic times, when the only meat available was wild game. Back in those times, the most abundant game was wild boar and deer. This is why so many recipes for pork and venison exist. These days, however, the deer population has been seriously depleted, and venison is not easily found. Wild boars still roam the forests of the Yucatán, but ever since the Spaniards introduced domesticated pigs, most people find it easier to raise pigs or buy pork, rather than hunt boar.

However, that is not to say that people don't hunt in the Yucatán. Many men in rural areas do hunt for their food, and despite the fact that boars and deer are getting scarce, they do manage to bring home good numbers of birds and iguanas. Driving through rural areas, it is not unusual to see nearly all of the men carrying large old rifles as they walk along the roads.

It is interesting, but typical of the culture, that although there is now a sizable beef industry in the Yucatán, little has found its way into the diet of the native population. Most of the beef raised in the Yucatán winds up being served as steaks or burgers to the tourists in Cancún and other popular tourist areas.

With all of the wonderful recipes for other meats or foods, it's easy to see why there is so little interest in beef. One of the most famous dishes from the Yucatán is *Cochinita Pibil*, pork cooked in the *pibil* style. Traditionally this dish called for wild boar to be covered with local seasonings and spices, wrapped in banana leaves, and cooked in a stone-lined, coal-filled pit. This method would bake and steam the boar at the same time, while infusing the meat with the flavor of the seasonings and spices, including the distinctively flavored banana leaves.

Cochinita Pibil remains one of the most popular dishes in the Yucatán despite the fact that it is generally not prepared in the traditional method. Ovens have replaced pits and domesticated pig has replaced wild boar. But the seasonings remain virtually the same and many restaurants still wrap the meat in banana leaves before cooking. We think that the results are absolutely delicious; *Cochinita Pibil* is one of our favorite foods from the Yucatán, and naturally we include a recipe for this tasty dish in this chapter.

Pork Cooked in the Pibil Method

Cochinita Pibil

This pre-Columbian dish is probably the best known food of the Maya. It is also one of the most popular entrees in the Yucatán, and is on virtually every menu. The Maya used wild boar for this dish until the Spanish introduced domesticated pigs.

10 whole black peppercorns
1/4 teaspoon cumin seeds
5 cloves garlic
3 tablespoons *Recado Rojo* (page 21) or substitute *achiote* paste
1 teaspoon dried oregano, Mexican preferred
2 bay leaves
1/3 cup bitter orange juice (see page 105) or substitute 1/3 cup lime juice, fresh preferred
2 pounds lean pork, cut in 1 1/2- or 2-inch cubes
String
3 fresh *xcatic* chiles, stems and seeds removed, cut in strips or substitute fresh banana or *güero* chiles
***Cebollas Encuridas* (page 23) or substitute sliced purple raw onions**
Banana leaves or aluminum foil

Place the peppercorns and cumin seeds in a spice or coffee grinder and process to a fine powder. Combine the powder with the garlic and place in a blender or food processor and purée.

Combine the spice mixture, *Recado Rojo* or *achiote* paste, oregano, bay leaves, and orange juice. Pour the marinade over the pork and marinate for 3 hours or overnight.

Cut two pieces of string long enough to fit around a roasting pan. Lay the strings on the bottom of the pan. Cut the banana leaves in pieces to fit the pan and line the pan with them.

Place the pork, including the marinade, on the leaves and top with the chiles and onions. Fold the banana leaves over the meat and tie with the strings. Cover the pan and bake in a 325 degree oven for 1 1/2 hours.

Serve with warmed corn tortillas, *Frijoles Negros* (page 87), additional *Cebollas Encuridas* (page 23), and a *habanero* salsa.

Yield: 4 to 6 servings

Note: This recipe requires advance preparation.

Yucatán Shredded Venison

Salpicón de Venado

Salpicón, "anything cut in small pieces," is a tasty way of using leftover meats. In the Yucatán, the traditional meat is venison cooked *pibil* style, but beef or even pork can be used. Serve this as a cold meat salad or as an interesting filling for tacos.

2 cups cooked, shredded venison or substitute beef
1/2 cup bitter orange juice (see page 105) or substitute 1/2 cup lime juice, fresh preferred
2 tomatoes, finely chopped
2/3 cup finely chopped radishes
3 tablespoons finely chopped fresh cilantro leaves
Salt to taste

Mix all of the ingredients together and let sit for an hour before serving.

Yield: 4 servings

Lamb Yucatán Style

Canero Estilo Yucateco

Like many local specialties, this dish can often be found in the local markets. Since there is usually no refrigeration in the markets, it's best to buy it early in the morning when it's fresh. It is often served on a bed of sieved *ibis*, a small locally grown white bean.

1 tablespoon *Recado Rojo* (page 21) or substitute *achiote* paste
2 tablespoons cider vinegar
2 pounds boneless lamb, cut into 1/2-inch cubes
1 small onion, finely chopped
2 fresh *chile dulce*, stem and seeds removed, finely chopped or substitute 1 small bell pepper
1 fresh *habanero* chile, stem and seeds removed, chopped or substitute 2 fresh jalapeño or 3 serrano chiles
4 cloves garlic, finely chopped
2 tablespoons vegetable oil
2 large tomatoes, chopped
2 cups water

Dilute the *Recado Rojo* or *achiote* paste with the vinegar and rub the marinade into the meat. Marinate for at least an hour.

Sauté the onion, peppers, and garlic in the oil for 5 minutes or until softened.

Place the meat in a saucepan along with the onion mixture. Add the tomatoes and water. Bring to a boil, reduce the heat and simmer, uncovered, until tender, about an hour.

Yield: 6 servings

Garlic Pork with Rice and Black Beans

Puerco Ajo Con Arroz Y Frijoles

This local version of pork and beans is a Monday night meal in many Yucatecan homes. It is also served with roasted tomato sauce, *Salsa de Jitomate*, over the top. Just add a salad or vegetable.

Beans

2 cups black beans
1 quart water
1 large onion, quartered
8 cloves garlic, coarsely chopped
1 tablespoon dried *epazote*
1 fresh *habanero* chile, stem and seeds removed and chopped or substitute 2 fresh jalapeño or 3 serrano chiles

Pork

2 pounds lean pork, cut into 1 1/2-inch cubes
1 small onion, chopped
2 tablespoons vegetable oil
2 tablespoons white vinegar
2 cups water
1 head garlic, roasted, peeled, and chopped
2 large tomatoes, roasted, peeled, and chopped
2 fresh serrano chiles, stems removed, sliced into rings
1 teaspoon dried oregano, Mexican preferred
1 teaspoon dried *epazote*
Freshly ground black pepper

Rice

1 cup long-grain rice
1 tablespoon vegetable oil
4 cloves garlic, roasted, peeled, and chopped
1 teaspoon ground cinnamon
2 cups bean liquid

1 avocado, sliced
***Salsa de Jitomate de Yuceteca* (page 26) optional**
***Cebollas Encuridas* (page 23) or substitute 1 small onion, sliced into rings**
***Salpicón* (page 24)**
Corn tortillas

Cover the beans with the water and soak overnight. Add the onion, garlic, *epazote*, and *habanero* chiles. Bring to a boil, reduce the heat and simmer until the beans are almost done, about 2 hours. Remove the onion and *epazote* if possible.

Sauté the pork and onion in the oil until browned. Remove the pork and place in a heavy kettle. Deglaze the pan with the vinegar. Pour 2 cups of water into the pan, and bring to a boil. Remove the pan and add the liquid to the pork mixture.

Add the garlic, tomatoes, chiles, oregano, *epazote*, pepper, a cup of the beans, and 2 cups of the bean liquid. Simmer until the pork is tender.

Brown the rice in the oil. Add the garlic and cinnamon. Measure 4 cups of the bean liquid into a saucepan and bring to a boil. Add the rice, bring back to a boil, reduce the heat, cover and simmer until the rice is done, about 20 minutes.

Reheat the remaining beans with some of the bean liquid until it has been reduced and thickened.

Place the rice in the middle of a large platter and the beans and sauce on one side and the beans and pork on the other side. Garnish the rice with the avocado slices. Pour the sauce over the pork or serve some of it on the side. The onions and *salpicón* can be used to garnish the pork or set out in a bowl. Serve this dish with warmed tortillas.

Yield: 4 to 6 servings

Note: This recipe requires advance preparation.

Yucatán Ribs

Costilla de Puerco Yucateca

This recipe for ribs comes from the Mérida area, where they are served with a plateful of lime wedges.

3 1/2 to 4 pounds pork spareribs or 1 pound thick pork chops
Juice of 4 limes

Sauce
2 dried ancho chiles, toasted, stems and seeds removed
Hot water, to cover
1 cup *Adobo Sauce* (page 22)
1/2 cup bitter orange juice (see page 105) or substitute 1/2 cup lime juice, fresh preferred
1/4 cup red wine vinegar
1/4 cup chopped fresh cilantro
1/4 teaspoon sugar

Rub the ribs with the lime juice and let sit for an hour.

Soak the chiles in hot water for 15 minutes or until soft. Drain them. Place the chiles and a little of the water that they were soaking in into a blender or food processor and purée until smooth. Combine with the remaining sauce ingredients.

Place the ribs on a rack, cover with foil, and bake in a 350 degree oven for 1 hour. Liberally baste the ribs with the sauce, and continue to bake, uncovered, for another hour or until they are done. At this point you could also place them over charcoal and grill until done.

Cut the ribs apart and serve.

Yield: 4 to 6 servings

Valladolid Smoked Sausage

Longaniza de Valladolid

This famous spicy, thin sausage from the Valladolid area is popular all over the Yucatán. Traditionally, an oil drum smoker is used to smoke it, but a backyard smoker will work as well or better.

1 tablespoon whole allspice berries
2 teaspoons whole black peppercorns
6 whole cloves
1/4 teaspoon cumin seeds
1 tablespoon dried oregano, Mexican preferred
2 teaspoons salt
2 tablespoons ground annatto seeds
1/3 cup white vinegar
8 cloves garlic, chopped
1 medium purple onion, finely chopped
1 pound boneless pork, very finely ground
4 tablespoons pork fat, very finely ground
8 12-inch lengths of narrow pork casings

Place the allspice, peppercorns, cloves, cumin, oregano, and salt in a spice or coffee grinder and process to a fine powder. Place the powder, annatto, vinegar, garlic, and onion and in a blender or food processor and purée until smooth.

Combine the meat, fat, and seasonings in a nonmetallic bowl and mix well. Cover and refrigerate for 12 hours.

Stuff the sausage casings, leaving about 1/2 inch empty at each end. Smooth the sausages out and twist both ends of each.

Slowly smoke in a smoker, following the manufacturer's directions.

Yield: 8 sausages

Note: This recipe requires advance preparation.

Steak en Poblano Chile Sauce

Bistec en Salsa de Chile Poblano

This nontraditional recipe is typical of the Cancún area, where Mexican ingredients are often combined with techniques and ingredients from around the world to produce exciting new dishes.

4 beefsteaks, tenderloin preferred
2 to 3 tablespoons vegetable oil
1 small onion, chopped
3 cloves garlic, chopped
1 cup beef broth
4 fresh *poblano* chiles, roasted, peeled, stems and seeds removed
1 cup heavy cream
Salt and pepper
1 cup shredded *Chihuahua* cheese or substitute Provolone or Monterey Jack cheese

Sauté the steaks in the oil to the desired doneness, about 6 to 7 minutes for medium rare. Remove and keep warm.

Pour off all but a tablespoon of the oil. Sauté the onion and garlic until browned. Add the broth, quickly bring to a boil and deglaze the pan.

Place 3 of the chiles and the onion mixture in a blender or food processor, and purée to a smooth sauce. Add the cream. Season with salt and pepper.

Return the sauce to the pan and simmer for 5 minutes to heat and thicken the sauce.

Cut the remaining chile in strips. Place the steaks on a platter, pour the sauce over them, and top with the chile strips and cheese. Put the steaks under the broiler until the cheese melts.

Yield: 4 servings

Meatballs in Chipotle Sauce

Albóndigas en Chipotle

Albóndigas, or meatballs, are found throughout Mexico and are used in soups, stews, or sauces such as this. They have their origins in the Middle East, were brought to Spain by the Muslims, and then were introduced to the New World by the Spaniards.

2 dried *chipotle* chiles, stems removed
Hot water, to cover
3 tomatoes, peeled, seeds removed, chopped
1 small onion, chopped
1 teaspoon dried *epazote*
3 tablespoons vegetable oil
2 cups beef broth
1/2 pound ground beef
1/2 pound ground pork
1 egg, beaten
1/4 cup finely chopped onion
1/4 cup dried bread crumbs
3 teaspoons ground allspice
1/4 teaspoon ground cinnamon

Soak the chiles in hot water for 15 minutes or until soft; drain them. Discard water. Place the chiles along with the tomatoes, onion, and *epazote* in a blender or food processor and purée until smooth.

Sauté the tomato purée in 1 tablespoon of the oil for 5 minutes. Stir in the beef broth. Simmer the sauce for 10 minutes.

Combine the beef, pork, egg, onion, bread crumbs, and spices. Mix well and form into small balls. Brown the meatballs in the remaining oil. Remove and drain.

Add the meatballs to the sauce and simmer for 15 or 20 minutes or until done.

Serve over rice, with a salad and warm tortillas.

Yield: 4 to 6 servings

Stuffed Pork Shoulder

Lomo de Puerco Relleno

Rellenos, or foods with stuffing, are very popular in this part of Mexico where cooks stuff not only chiles, but also poultry and meat. Don't let the list of ingredients scare you off—this recipe is not as difficult as it appears.

Sauce

4 dried ancho chiles, stems and seeds removed
Hot water, to cover
1 medium onion, chopped
4 cloves garlic, chopped
1 tablespoon vegetable oil
2 large tomatoes, peeled and chopped
1/4 cup white vinegar
2 teaspoons chopped fresh cilantro
1 teaspoon ground cinnamon
1/4 teaspoon ground allspice
2 cups water

Filling

4 ounces pork sausage
1 large onion, sliced
6 cloves garlic, chopped
1 potato, peeled and cubed
2 fresh *poblano* chiles, roasted, peeled, stems and seeds removed, chopped
1 cup cooked, chopped *chaya* leaves or substitute spinach
2 hard-cooked eggs, peeled and chopped
2 eggs, beaten
1 4-pound pork shoulder roast, butterflied

Cover the anchos with hot water and soak for 15 minutes or until softened. Drain. Discard the water.

Sauté the onion and garlic in the oil. Stir in the remaining sauce ingredients and simmer for 10 minutes. Put the mixture in a blender or food processor along with the anchos and purée until smooth. Strain if necessary.

Brown the sausage, onion, and garlic until the sausage is done. Combine with the potato, *poblano* chiles, *chaya*, and hard-cooked eggs and mix well. Stir in the beaten eggs.

Place the stuffing on the meat and roll up. Tie the roast securely with string in at least four places.

Place the roast on a rack, pour the sauce over the top and bake in a 350 degree oven for 40 to 45 minutes per pound, or to an internal temperature of 185 degrees, basting occasionally with the sauce. Cover the pan if the roast is browning too much. Let the roast sit for 20 minutes, and then slice.

Strain the pan drippings and pour over the pork. Serve with extra sauce on the side.

Yield: 6 to 8 servings

Chicken and Pork Tamale Pie

Muc-bil Pollo

This very old Mayan recipe is traditionally prepared for the dead on All Saints Day and was described by John L. Stephens in his classic book from the 1800s, *Incidents of Travel in Yucatán.*

Filling

1/2 pound boneless pork, cut in 1-inch cubes
2 boneless chicken breasts
2 tablespoons ground annatto seeds
2 large onions, chopped, divided
4 cloves garlic, chopped
2 teaspoons dried oregano, Mexican preferred, divided
Water, to cover

Sauce

3 tomatoes, peeled, seeds removed, chopped
2 cups chicken broth
1 fresh *habanero* chile, stem and seeds removed, chopped or substitute 2 fresh jalapeño or 3 serrano chiles
3 tablespoons white vinegar
2 tablespoons *Recado Rojo* (page 21) or substitute *achiote* paste
1 teaspoon dried *epazote*
1/2 teaspoon ground cumin

Topping

3 cups *masa harina*
1 1/2 cups broth (reserved broth plus more chicken broth added if necessary)
1/4 cup shortening

Banana leaves or aluminum foil

Combine the pork, chicken, annatto, 1/2 of the onion, garlic, and 1 teaspoon of the oregano in a pot and cover with water. Bring to a boil, reduce the heat, and simmer until the pork is done, about 40 minutes. Remove the meat and chop the chicken. Strain the broth and reserve.

Place the tomatoes, broth, chiles, vinegar, *Recado Rojo* or *achiote* paste, remaining onion and oregano, *epazote*, and cumin in a blender or food processor and purée until smooth.

Slowly add the broth to the *masa*. Cream the shortening until light and fluffy. Add the *masa* and continue to beat.

Lay the leaves in a shallow, 10- x 7-inch pan. Press half of the *masa* on the bottom of the pan. Add the meats and pour the sauce over. Press the remaining *masa* over the meat, fold the leaves over, and cover the pan.

Bake in a 350 degree oven for 45 minutes or until the topping is done.

Yield: 6 servings

Poultry

Just a glance at a menu from a Yucatecan restaurant that features regional food will show the importance of poultry to the area: typically at least half of the meals offered will feature poultry. Turkey is favored over chicken for historical reasons, although the two have become interchangeable to some extent. Indigenous to the Yucatán, turkeys and pheasants were highly prized by the ancient Maya, who created many appealing recipes for them. However, since turkeys are easily domesticated, they have become far more numerous and more popular than pheasant, which is now considered a delicacy.

Some of the oldest recipes in the area are for turkeys with many different complex and spicy stuffings. We tend to think of variations of bread stuffing when we consider stuffing a turkey, while the Maya use a wide variety of ingredients including everything from meats to fruits and vegetables, everything except bread. They also have many other unusual methods of preparing and serving turkey, a number of which we include in this chapter.

Introduced to the Maya by the Spaniards, chickens have become nearly as popular as turkeys. *Pollo Pibil*, chicken cooked in the *pibil* style, is one of the most famous and most delicious dishes in the Yucatán. Chicken eggs also play an important role in the cuisine, especially hard-cooked eggs, which are a major ingredient in many popular Yucatecan dishes. It is really impossible to overstate the role of poultry in the Yucatán, since without it there would hardly be an identifiable cuisine.

Driving through rural areas in the Yucatán is another way to see just how important poultry is, because every home has a flock of chickens, and almost all have at least one turkey. Because they are free-ranging, they tend to be tougher but more flavorful than those raised in confinement. This is also true for wild turkeys and is why most of the cooking methods for poultry involve moist heat, including poaching, simmering, and steaming. Some of those birds are probably a bit chewy by the time they get caught, and slow cooking in a moist heat will help make them more palatable.

These days it seems that everyone has one hundred and one ways to fix chicken, and most of them sound either boring or inedible to anyone with working taste buds. We have had our eyes opened by the variety of poultry recipes that we found in the Yucatán and hope that you will find the following recipes as interesting and appetizing as we did.

Spiced Chicken Valladolid Style

Pollo Escabeche de Valladolid

Also known as *Pollo Escabeche Oriental*, this very popular chicken dish reflects a Spanish influence in its use of seasonings and vinegar.

4 chicken legs and thighs
2 cups chicken broth
4 cups water
1/2 teaspoon dried oregano, Mexican preferred
1/4 teaspoon coarsely ground black pepper
8 whole allspice berries
2 cloves garlic, minced
1/2 cup *Recado de Bistec* (page 21), divided or Xak (page 23)
All-purpose flour for dusting
Vegetable oil
2 tablespoons white vinegar
4 fresh *xcatic* chiles, roasted, peeled, cut in strips or substitute fresh banana or *güero* chiles
1 large onion, roasted, cut in wedges

Cover the chicken with the broth and water. Bring to a boil, reduce the heat and simmer for 5 minutes, skimming off any foam that forms. Add the oregano, black pepper, allspice, and garlic. Continue to simmer for 25 minutes or until the chicken is done. Allow the chicken to cool in the broth, remove, and strain the broth.

Rub all but 1 tablespoon of the *Recado de Bistec* into the chicken and then dust lightly with the flour. Oil a griddle and fry the chicken until browned, about 3 to 4 minutes per side. Remove and drain.

Reheat 4 cups of the broth. Stir in the remaining *Recado de Bistec* and the vinegar.

Divide the chiles and onions in 4 soup bowls and pour the broth over the top. Place a piece of chicken in each bowl and serve.

Yield: 4 servings

Chicken Cooked in the Pibil Method

Pollo Pibil

This uniquely Yucatecan dish is available in nearly every restaurant there that features local cuisine. Originally cooked over coals in pits dug in the ground, *pollo pibil* is most often baked in ovens these days. We have had great success in duplicating the pit method by using an inexpensive backyard smoker. We don't add any wood chips for smoke. We use a pan of water between the coals and the wrapped chicken to keep the chicken juicy. Serve with black beans (*Frijoles Negros*, page 87), pickled onions (*Cebollas Encuridas*, page 23), and *habanero* salsa for a truly authentic meal.

1/4 cup *Recado Rojo* (page 21) or substitute *achiote* paste
1/2 cup bitter orange juice (page 105) or substitute orange juice
4 chicken breasts, skin removed
1 medium onion, sliced
3 fresh *xcatic* chiles, stems and seeds removed, chopped or substitute fresh banana or *güero* chiles
1 tablespoon vegetable oil
Banana leaves or aluminum foil
4 sprigs fresh *epazote* or substitute 1 tablespoon dried *epazote*
4 tablespoons margarine

Mix the *Recado Rojo* or *achiote* paste with the orange juice. Prick the chicken breasts with a fork and pour the marinade over the chicken. Marinate in the refrigerator for 4 to 6 hours or overnight.

Sauté the onion and chiles in the oil until soft.

Line a roasting pan with the banana leaves. Place the chicken on the leaves, pour over the remaining marinade, and top with the onions and chiles. Place a little *epazote* on each breast along with a tablespoon of margarine. Fold the leaves over, cover the pan and bake at 350 degrees for an hour.

Yield: 4 servings

Note: This recipe requires advance preparation.

Motul Chicken

Pollo de Motul

This recipe is named after the town of Motul outside of Mérida. Traditionally the meat should be shredded, but we prefer to serve the pieces whole with the sauce over the top.

Marinade

1 dried ancho chile, stem and seeds removed
Hot water, to cover
1 teaspoon whole allspice berries
1/2 teaspoon cumin seed
1 teaspoon dried oregano, Mexican preferred
1 small onion, chopped
3/4 cup bitter orange juice (page 105) or substitute grapefruit juice
1 chicken, cut into quarters

Tomato Sauce

6 tomatillos, either fresh or canned, rinsed
3 fresh serrano chiles, roasted, peeled, stems removed, chopped
1 cup cooked peas
6 ounces ham, diced
1/2 cup crumbled *queso asadero* cheese or substitute provolone cheese

Soak the ancho in hot water for 15 minutes or until soft. Drain. Discard water.

Place the allspice and cumin in a spice or coffee grinder and process to a fine powder. Place the powder, ancho, oregano, onion, and orange juice in a blender or food processor and purée until smooth. Cover the chicken with the mixture and marinate in the refrigerator for 4 to 6 hours or overnight.

Bake the chicken, along with the marinade, in a 350 degree oven for 30 to 40 minutes or until done. Remove the chicken and keep warm.

If using fresh tomatillos, remove the husks and simmer for 10 to 15 minutes or until they turn light green and are soft. Drain.

Place in a blender or food processor along with the serranos and purée until smooth. Sauté the sauce in 1 tablespoon of oil for 5 minutes.

Place the chicken on a serving platter or individual plates. Pour the tomatillo sauce over the chicken, top with the peas and ham, garnish with the cheese and serve.

Yield: 4 to 6 servings

Note: This recipe requires advance preparation.

Pichones en Pipián Rojo

Pheasant in Red Pipián Sauce

Pheasants are available in the Yucatán and are featured in many recipes. *Pipián* refers to a sauce that is thickened with either seeds or nuts and is probably one of the earliest *moles*. Pumpkin seeds are traditionally used, but if they are not available, substitute nuts, such as almonds.

2 pheasants or substitute 4 cornish game hens
Salt and pepper
6 strips bacon
1 dried ancho chile, stem and seeds removed
2 dried *pasilla* chiles, stems and seeds removed
Hot water, to cover
1 small onion, chopped
2 cloves garlic, chopped
2 medium tomatoes, peeled and seeded, chopped
1/2 teaspoon ground cinnamon
1/2 teaspoon ground allspice
1/4 teaspoon ground annatto seeds
2 cups chicken broth
1 cup toasted ground *pepitas* (pumpkin seeds)

Season the cavities of the pheasants with salt and pepper. Cover the breasts with the bacon as they tend to dry out when baking. Bake in a 350 degree oven for 30 to 45 minutes or until done, basting frequently with the juices.

Soak the chiles in hot water for 15 minutes or until soft. Drain. Discard water.

Place the chiles, onion, garlic and tomatoes in the blender or food processor and purée to a smooth sauce. Add the cinnamon, allspice, annatto, and broth and blend again. Slowly stir in the *pepitas* by hand.

Simmer the sauce until thickened, about 15 minutes. Do not allow it to boil or it will separate.

To serve, carve the pheasants, place on a serving platter and top with the sauce. If using cornish hens, place on plates and top with sauce.

Yield: 4 servings

Turkey in Almond Sauce

Pavo en Salsa de Almendras

This dish is traditionally served with fried, cubed French bread and plantains as a garnish, although it is just as tasty without the bread. Plantains are often hard to find north of the border, so we have substituted bananas.

3/4 cup blanched almonds
1/2 teaspoon dried oregano, Mexican preferred
1/2 teaspoon whole black peppercorns
2 medium onions, roasted, peeled, and chopped, divided
3 fresh *xcatic* chiles, stems and seeds removed, roasted, peeled, and chopped, divided or substitute fresh banana or *güero* chiles
1 head of garlic, roasted, peeled, and chopped, divided
2 tablespoons white vinegar
3 1/2 cups water, divided
2 turkey thighs or substitute 4 chicken breasts
Vegetable oil for frying
1 large banana, peeled and cut into 1/2-inch rounds

Place the almonds, oregano, and peppercorns in a spice or coffee grinder and process to a fine powder. Place the powder, half the onions, chile, garlic, vinegar, and 1/2 cup of water in a blender or food processor and purée until the mixture is the consistency of a smooth paste.

Spread half of the almond mixture over the turkey pieces and marinate for a minimum of 2 hours or overnight in the refrigerator.

Pour about an inch of oil in the bottom of a skillet and heat to 325 degrees. Sauté the turkey pieces very lightly, being careful that the almond coating doesn't burn. Remove the turkey and set aside to drain off any remaining oil.

Pour off excess oil and add the remaining garlic, onions, and chiles to the pan along with the turkey pieces. Add about 3 cups of water, cover, and simmer until the turkey is done, about 35 to 45 minutes. Remove them and keep warm.

Stir the remaining almond paste into the sauce and simmer for 10 minutes to thicken.

To serve, place the turkey on a serving platter, top with the additional sauce, arrange the bananas around the turkey, and serve.

Yield: 6 servings

Note: This recipe requires advance preparation.

Cold Spiced Turkey

Pavo en Frio

While it may seem a little bizarre to boil or poach a turkey (it certainly did to us), we have to admit that the results are well worth the effort. Although this recipe looks and sounds complicated, it really isn't. Serve sliced as a cold appetizer or entree; it also makes great sandwiches.

1 4-pound turkey breast
3 ounces ham, cut into strips
1 tablespoon whole black peppercorns
8 cloves garlic (4 slivered, 4 left whole)
1 tablespoon ground cinnamon
1 tablespoon ground nutmeg
1 tablespoon ground cloves
2 teaspoons ground allspice
Cheesecloth
1 small onion, quartered
2 bay leaves
Water, to cover
2 cups dry white wine
2 oranges, sectioned
1/2 cup bitter orange juice (page 105) or substitute 1/2 cup lime juice, fresh preferred
2 tablespoons white vinegar

Sauce
1/2 cup olive oil
1/4 cup red wine vinegar

Make deep slits in the turkey with a knife and insert the ham, peppercorns, and slivers of garlic. Combine the cinnamon, nutmeg, cloves, and allspice and rub the outside of the turkey with the mixture and let sit at room temperature for 1/2 hour. Wrap the turkey with a double thickness of cheesecloth and securely tie.

Place the turkey in a large pot, add the onion, the whole cloves of garlic, bay leaves, and enough water to cover by an inch. Bring to a boil, reduce the heat, cover and lightly simmer for an hour. Remove the turkey and strain the stock.

Return the turkey to the pot, add 4 cups of the reserved stock, wine, orange sections, orange juice, and white vinegar. Cover and cook over medium heat for another hour or until the turkey is tender.

Remove the turkey and let cool at room temperature for 30 minutes or until completely cooled. Remove the cheesecloth and skin. Slice the turkey and place on a platter.

Strain the broth and measure out 1 cup. Whisk with the oil and vinegar to make a dressing and serve on the side.

Yield: 8 to 10 servings

Note: The excess broth can be saved and used as a base for soup or an unusual gravy.

Turkey Served with Black Sauce

Chilmole

We have been served chilmole in a variety of ways: as a single, large meatball or as shredded turkey in a black sauce, or as a stuffed turkey with ground pork, tomatoes, and eggs. The following recipe is an easy version that is made with a turkey leg and thigh. Glossy black in appearance, it is hardly an appetizing-looking dish. It is, however, extremely rich and delicious, and well worth the effort to make it.

2 turkey legs and thighs
4 cups chicken broth
6 whole allspice berries
4 cloves garlic
1 teaspoon *epazote*
1/4 teaspoon cumin seeds
1/4 teaspoon dried oregano, Mexican preferred
1/2 cup *Recado de Chilmole* (page 22)
1 tablespoon flour
4 hard-cooked eggs, peeled, cut in wedges

Place the turkey in a large pot and add the broth. Bring to a boil, reduce the heat and simmer for 5 minutes, skimming off the foam that forms. Add the allspice, garlic, *epazote*, cumin, and oregano and simmer for 35 to 40 minutes or until the turkey is done. Remove the meat and cool. Strain the broth and skim off any excess fat. Reserve the broth.

When the turkey is cool, remove the skin and discard. Using two forks, shred the turkey meat.

Reheat the broth and stir in the *recado* and simmer for 20 minutes. Thicken the sauce, if needed, by mixing the flour with a little of the broth and then slowly adding it to the sauce.

To serve, place the turkey in a serving bowl, top with the sauce and garnish with the egg wedges.

Yield: 4 to 6 servings

Stuffed Turkey with White Sauce

Pavo en Relleno Blanco

The spicy stuffing of this dish is an excellent complement to the turkey. This traditional dish is served with a white sauce instead of a gravy.

Stuffing

1 pound ground pork
1 onion, chopped
4 tomatoes, peeled and chopped
4 fresh *xcatic* chiles, stems and seeds removed, chopped or substitute fresh banana or *güero* chiles
8 cloves garlic, chopped
2 tablespoons dried oregano, Mexican preferred
1 tablespoon dried cilantro
1 tablespoon ground allspice
2 teaspoons ground cinnamon
3/4 teaspoon ground cloves
1/2 teaspoon ground cumin
1/4 teaspoon saffron
1/2 cup stuffed green olives
1/2 cup toasted almonds, chopped
1/3 cup raisins
1/4 cup capers
2 eggs, beaten
4 hard-cooked eggs, peeled and chopped
4 tablespoons white vinegar

1 6- to 7-pound turkey

Gravy

3 tablespoons all-purpose flour
3 cups chicken broth

Sauté the pork until browned. Add the onion, tomatoes, chiles, garlic, oregano, and cilantro and simmer for 3 to 5 minutes.

Combine the allspice, cinnamon, cloves, cumin, and saffron. Add all but a teaspoon of the spices to the meat mixture. Mix all of the remaining ingredients, except the vinegar, and add to the stuffing.

Stuff the turkey with the mixture and place on a roasting rack breast side up. Whisk the remaining teaspoon of spices with the vinegar and rub into the turkey.

Place in a 450 degree oven and immediately reduce the heat to 350 degrees. Roast, basting frequently with the pan drippings, until done, approximately 20 minutes per pound. Remove the turkey and keep warm.

To make the gravy, heat the pan drippings and stir in the flour and simmer until dissolved. Whisk in the broth, increase the heat, and cook, stirring constantly, until the sauce has thickened.

Yield: 6 to 8 servings

Eggs Motuleños Style

Huevos Motuleños

The addition of ham and peas is unusual, but typical of the Motul way of cooking. This is the Yucatecan version of *huevos rancheros* and is extremely popular throughout the peninsula.

3 tomatoes, peeled and chopped
1 medium onion, chopped
2 cloves garlic
1/2 cup chicken broth
1 fresh *habanero* chile, stem and seeds removed, chopped or substitute 2 fresh jalapeño or 3 serrano chiles
2 tablespoons vegetable oil
4 ounces chorizo sausage
4 corn tortillas
Vegetable oil for frying
4 eggs
1 cup heated *Frijoles Negros* (page 87)
1 cup cooked peas
1 1/2 cups boiled ham, chopped
2 cups crumbled *queso fresco* or substitute Monterey Jack cheese

Place the tomatoes, onion, and garlic in a blender and purée until smooth, adding some broth if necessary. Sauté the mixture along with the chiles in the oil. Add the remaining broth and simmer until the sauce has thickened.

Crumble and fry the chorizo until done. Add to the chile sauce.

Fry the tortillas in oil for a couple of seconds to soften, making sure they do not become crisp. Remove and drain.

Fry the eggs in the oil that the tortillas were fried in.

Place a tortilla on a plate and cover with the beans. Place the egg on the beans, pour the sauce over the egg. Garnish with the peas, ham, and cheese and serve.

Yield: 4 servings

Tortilla Strip Casserole

Chilaquiles

This dish, which means "broken-up sombrero" because it has torn (or broken) tortillas as a base, makes a tasty and easy-to-prepare breakfast or brunch. It is also a good way to use leftovers and stale tortillas.

3 dried ancho chiles, stems and seeds removed
Hot water, to cover
3 large tomatoes, roasted, peeled and chopped
1 medium onion, roasted, peeled and chopped
1 cup heavy cream
12 corn tortillas, cut in wedges
Vegetable oil for frying
3 cups cooked, shredded chicken
1 small onion, sliced in thin rings
1/4 cup grated cheese *queso fresco* or substitute Monterey Jack cheese

Cover the chiles with hot water and let them sit for 15 minutes until softened. Drain.

Place the chiles, tomatoes, onion, and cream in a blender and purée until smooth. Simmer the sauce for 15 or 20 minutes to thicken.

Fry the tortillas in the oil until chewy but not crisp.

Place a layer of the tortillas on a plate and then a layer of chicken. Cover with the sauce, top with the onions and cheese.

Yield: 4 servings

Fish

On a recent trip to the Yucatán, we spent a morning out on the Celestún Estuary, viewing the huge flocks of Greater Flamingos. Afterwards we headed into town to find lunch. Celestún is a tiny little fishing town, with a couple of rustic hotels, and a short line of restaurants on the beach. We sat out under cover on the front porch of the Restaurant Celestún and had a cool drink while checking out both the incredible menu and the lovely sea and beach in front of us.

The restaurant menu was a seafood lover's delight. Our only problem was trying to decide exactly what we wanted and how much we thought we could eat. We finally decided to split a large shrimp cocktail as an appetizer, and for entrées, ordered one plate of grilled shrimp and a second of stone crab claws. It was a spectacular meal, almost more than we could finish, but we managed to eat every bite. It was served with lots of tart lime wedges, which added the perfect touch when squeezed liberally over all three dishes. Of course, when starting with shrimp and crab that has only been out of the sea for a few hours, it's hard to go too far wrong. Regardless, that was a seafood feast that would have been awarded 5 stars from every guidebook ever written.

This is not an unusual occurrence in the Yucatán, which has nearly 1000 miles of seacoast. The Caribbean to the east and the Gulf of Mexico to the west yield up an array of seafood that can please any seafood lover. The list of seafood available seems endless and includes shrimp, crab, lobster, shark, shellfish, mollusks like squid and octopus, and wonderfully tasty fish such as snapper, grouper, pompano, tuna, bass, halibut, mackerel, barracuda, and many more.

Not only is there an incredible variety of seafood available, there are also a wide number of ways to prepare it. One of the most popular seafood dishes in the Yucatán is ceviche, which many people consider raw fish. Actually ceviche is seafood that has been "cooked" by an acid, which in the Yucatán is usually lime juice. By cutting the raw seafood into small pieces and allowing it to marinate for at least four hours, it does get cooked as evidenced by the fact that it turns from translucent to opaque. Adding onions, chiles, and cilantro makes this one of the tastiest of all seafood treats!

Pescado en Tikin Xik, or fish prepared in the *pibil* style, is a unique Yucatecan method of cooking seafood. Similar to *Cochinita* and *Pollo Pibil* in preparation, fish cooked *pibil* style is covered with *achiote* paste, tomatoes, onions, and chile, wrapped in banana leaves, and baked. The results can only be described as heavenly. An extremely popular and tasty shark dish, *Pan de Cazón*, is served throughout the peninsula, although we have been told that the restaurants in Campeche serve the best. Another Yucatecan favorite is fish sautéed in butter and garlic, which is wonderful if you're a garlic lover. Seafood is also used to stuff chiles, as a filling in tamales, and in a variety of soups. As you can see, if you're a seafood lover, you can easily get your fill in the Yucatán and still have not tried everything.

Ceviche from Quintana Roo

De Punta Nizuc, Quintana Roo

Fish "cooked" in an acid-based liquid like lime juice is popular wherever there is seafood in Mexico. This dish, which we were served in Cancún, is a variation of the more typical fish, onion, and chile ceviche.

1/2 pound firm whitefish, such as snapper, pompano, or bass, cut in 1/2-inch cubes
1/2 pound small whole scallops
1 cup bitter orange juice (see page 105) or substitute 1 cup lime juice, fresh preferred
1 fresh *habanero* chile, stem and seeds removed, minced or substitute 2 fresh jalapeño or 3 serrano chiles
1 cup fresh pineapple, cut in chunks
1 small banana, sliced
3 tablespoons chopped roasted peanuts
3 tablespoons minced fresh cilantro

Combine the fish, scallops, orange juice, and chile in a nonmetallic bowl and refrigerate for 4 hours, turning occasionally until the fish loses its translucency and turns opaque.

Just before serving, drain the fish, toss with the fruit and place in parfait glasses. Garnish with the peanuts and cilantro, and serve.

Yield: 6 to 8 servings

Note: This recipe requires advance preparation.

Yucatecan Shrimp Cocktail

Coctel de Camarones Yucateca

We loved the way Yucatecans served seafood cocktails in tall parfait glasses with a thin sauce that was more like a juice. The chopped onions, cilantro, and habaneros were served separately so that everyone could add just as much or as little as they wanted.

2 large tomatoes, roasted, peeled, seeds removed, chopped
4 tablespoons bitter orange juice (see page 105) or substitute 4 tablespoons lime juice, fresh preferred
2 tablespoons olive oil
1 teaspoon sugar
1/2 cup minced purple onion, divided
Salt and freshly ground black pepper
1 pound cooked shrimp, shelled and deveined
1/4 cup minced fresh cilantro
1 fresh *habanero* chile, stem and seeds removed, minced or substitute 2 fresh jalapeño or 3 serrano chiles

Put the tomatoes, orange juice, and oil in a blender or food processor and purée until smooth. Stir in the sugar and 1/2 of the onion and season with salt and pepper. Simmer for 10 minutes and then cool.

Fill parfait glasses with the shrimp and add the juice until covered. Place the remaining onion, cilantro, and chiles on a plate and serve on the side.

Yield: 4 to 6 servings

Marinated Shrimp

Camarones en Escabeche

Pickling or "sousing" foods is common in the Yucatán and this popular dish is a good example. Serve these shrimp as an appetizer, salad or even an entree on a hot summer day.

1/4 cup olive oil, divided
2 pounds raw shrimp
3 cloves garlic, chopped
2 fresh *chile dulce*, stems and seeds removed, cut in strips, divided or substitute 1/2 cup sliced bell pepper
1 fresh *habanero* chile, stem and seeds removed, chopped or substitute 2 fresh jalapeño or 3 serrano chiles
1 large onion, thinly sliced
1/4 cup cooked peas
1/4 cup cooked carrots, cut in coins
3 whole cloves
1 teaspoon dried oregano
1 1-inch stick cinnamon
3/4 cup white vinegar
2 bay leaves

Heat half of the oil in a pan, add the shrimp, garlic, and half of the *chile dulce* and *habanero*. Sauté the mixture until the shrimp turns pink. Remove the shrimp, cool and peel.

Heat the remaining oil and sauté the onion until softened.

Combine the shrimp, most of the remaining chiles, peas, onions and carrots in a bowl.

Put the cloves, oregano, and cinnamon in a spice or coffee grinder and process to a fine powder. Place the powder and vinegar in a blender or food processor and purée until smooth.

Place the mixture in a saucepan, add the bay leaves, and bring to a boil. Pour over the shrimp mixture and marinate, in the refrigerator, for 4 hours.

To serve, drain the liquid and place the shrimp on a bed of greens. Garnish with the rest of the chile strips and serve.

Yield : 6 to 8 servings

Note: This recipe requires advance preparation.

Grouper Baked in Achiote Marinade

Pescado en Tikin Xik

Although the words "tikin xik" are Mayan meaning dried chile, this is not at all a fiery dish. It is instead a complexly flavored entrée that has become our favorite Yucatecan fish dish. Offered throughout the Yucatán, it is prepared with either whole fish or fillets, and can be either baked or grilled over charcoal.

1 whole grouper, snapper, or pollack or 2 fish steaks such as halibut
2 cloves garlic
1/4 teaspoon dried oregano
1/4 teaspoon cumin seeds
2 tablespoons *Recado Rojo* (page 21) or substitute *achiote* paste
1/4 cup bitter orange juice (see page 105) or substitute 1/4 cup lime juice, fresh preferred
Banana leaves or aluminum foil
1 large tomato, sliced
1/2 onion, sliced in rings and separated
2 fresh *xcatic* chiles, stems and seeds removed, sliced or substitute banana or *güero* chiles
12 green olives, sliced
3 tablespoons butter or margarine

If the fish is whole, clean it both inside and out. Make shallow slits in the fish so that the *Recado Rojo* will penetrate.

Put the garlic, oregano, and cumin seeds in a blender or food processor and purée. Add the *Recado Rojo* or *achiote* paste and orange juice and blend to a smooth paste. Rub some of the paste on both sides of the fish and let marinate for 2 hours.

Line a roasting pan with the leaves or foil. Lay the fish on the leaves and top with the remaining paste. Layer the tomato slices, onion slices, chiles, olives, and pieces of the butter or margarine. Fold the leaves over and cover the pan with a lid.

Bake in a 325 degree oven for 30 minutes.

Yield: 2 servings

Variation

Fillet the fish or open the fish out flat by removing the backbone. Proceed as above, letting the fish marinate for 2 hours. Lay the fish on a grill, basting with the remaining paste, and grill over coals until done, about 20 minutes.

Chiles Stuffed with Seafood

Chiles Rellenos de Mariscos

We enjoyed these unusual rellenos in a restaurant in Ticul set up behind the owner's home. Although this recipe calls for a mixture of seafood, a single ingredient such as shrimp works just as well.

1/4 cup minced onion
2 cloves garlic, minced
2 fresh *habanero* chiles, stems and seeds removed, minced or substitute 3 fresh jalapeño or 4 serrano chiles
1 tablespoon butter or margarine
1 pound mixed cooked seafood, such as shrimp, scallops, and calamari, diced
3 tablespoons chopped fresh cilantro
1 teaspoon dried oregano, Mexican preferred
4 tablespoons *Xnipek Salsa* (page 24) or substitute your favorite commercial salsa
4 fresh *poblano* chiles, roasted and peeled
Flour for dredging
3 eggs separated
1 tablespoon water
3 tablespoons flour
1/4 teaspoon salt
Vegetable oil for frying
***Salsa de Jitomate Yucateca* (page 26)**

Sauté the onion, garlic, and *habanero* in the butter until softened. Toss with the seafood, cilantro, oregano, and salsa.

Make a slit in the side of each *poblano* chile, and stuff the chiles with the seafood mixture. Dredge the chiles with the flour.

Beat the egg whites until they form stiff peaks.

Beat the yolks with the water, flour, and salt until thick and creamy. Fold the yolks into the whites.

Dip the chiles in the mixture until covered and then fry in 2 to 3 inches of oil until they are golden brown. Drain.

Serve with heated *Salsa de Jitomate Yucateca* on the side.

Yield: 4 servings

Grilled Shrimp in Achiote Sauce

Camarones Yucatecos

Although it may appear to be a good idea to baste the shrimp with leftover sauce while grilling, it is strongly flavored and can easily overpower the taste of the shrimp. So curb your instincts and grill the shrimp without basting. Serve as an appetizer or over plain white rice as an entree.

1 tablespoon vegetable oil
4 cloves garlic, chopped
2/3 cup bitter orange juice (see page 105) or substitute 2/3 cup lime juice, fresh preferred
1 tablespoon white vinegar
Water
1 teaspoon cumin seeds
1 1-inch stick cinnamon
4 whole cloves
10 whole black peppercorns
1 small onion, chopped
1 1/2 tablespoons *Recado Rojo* (page 21) or substitute *achiote* paste
1 pound large shrimp, shelled and deveined

Heat the oil and sauté the garlic until it is light brown. Allow to cool.

Combine the orange juice, vinegar, and add enough water to make 1 cup.

Place the cumin, cinnamon, cloves, and peppercorns in a spice or coffee grinder and process to a fine powder. Combine the powder, oil and garlic with the orange juice mixture, spices, onion, and *Recado Rojo* or *achiote* paste and purée to a smooth sauce in a blender or food processor.

Pour mixture into a large bowl, add the shrimp, and stir to coat well. Cover and let marinate in refrigerator overnight.

Thread the shrimp on skewers. (If using bamboo, soak in water for 15 minutes before using.) Grill or place under a broiler and cook until done.

Yield: 6 servings

Note: This recipe requires advance preparation.

Yucatecan Rice with Crab

Arroz Con Jaibas

This substantial dish can be a meal in itself; just serve with a green vegetable, hot tortillas, and *Agua Fresca* (page 103).

2 cups long-grain rice
2 tablespoons olive oil
1 large onion, chopped
2 cloves garlic, chopped
3 medium tomatoes, peeled, seeds removed, chopped
2 tablespoons *Recado Rojo* (page 21) or substitute *achiote* paste
4 cups chicken stock, divided
Salt and freshly ground pepper
1 1/2 pounds crabmeat, broken up
2 fresh *poblano* chiles, roasted, peeled, stems and seeds removed, chopped
1 bay leaf
1 cup raw peas
1/2 cup white wine

Sauté the rice in the oil and stir until it starts to brown.

Place the onion, garlic, tomatoes, *Recado Rojo* or *achiote* paste, and 1/2 cup of stock in a blender or food processor and purée until smooth.

Measure onion mixture and add enough stock to make 6 cups. Pour over rice; add salt and pepper to taste, crabmeat, *poblanos*, bay leaf, and peas.

Cover and cook in 350 degree oven for 30 minutes or until all the liquid has been absorbed. At this point, stir wine in gently so as not to break up the crabmeat, and put back in oven just long enough to heat thoroughly.

Yield: 6 to 8 servings

Tortillas Layered with Shark

Pan de Cazón

Cazón is a small shark that is very popular in the Yucatán, although any whitefish that is firm enough to shred can be used for this recipe. This can best be described as a fish pie, very typical of the Campeche area.

Filling

1 pound shark, halibut, or swordfish steaks
Water, to cover
1 onion, coarsely chopped
2 bay leaves
2 cloves garlic, chopped
1 tablespoon dried oregano, Mexican preferred

Sauce

1 fresh *habanero* chile, stem and seeds removed, chopped or substitute 2 fresh jalapeño or 3 serrano chiles
1 tablespoon dried *epazote*
4 cups *Salsa de Jitomate Yucateca* (page 26)

16 corn tortillas
2 cups warm *Frijoles Negros* (page 87)
4 whole *habanero* chiles for garnish

Cover the fish with water, add the onion, bay leaves, garlic, and oregano. Bring to a boil, reduce the heat and simmer for 10 minutes or until the fish is done. Remove the fish and cool.

Remove skin and bones from the fish and, using two forks, shred.

Add the chile and *epazote* to the tomato sauce. Simmer for 15 minutes to thicken. Remove the *epazote*.

To assemble, dip a tortilla into the sauce and place on a warmed platter. On the tortilla, spread a layer of the beans, then fish. Repeat the procedure with a second and third tortilla ending with a fourth tortilla on top. Make 3 more pies the same way.

Pour additional sauce over the top, garnish with a *habanero* and serve.

Yield: 4 servings

Shrimp Stuffed Pompano

Pámpano Pohchuc

This outstanding dish can easily be varied to suit individual tastes. Substitute other shellfish or chopped squid for the shrimp, and add cooked, diced vegetables such as potatoes, carrots, or peas.

1/2 teaspoon dried oregano, Mexican preferred
1/4 teaspoon ground cumin
4 cloves garlic
2 tablespoons olive oil
1 tablespoon *Recado Rojo* (page 21) or substitute *achiote* paste
1 1/2 to 2 pounds whole pompano, scaled and cleaned

Filling
1/4 pound shrimp, chopped
1/4 cup chopped onion
3 cloves garlic, minced
1 tablespoon olive oil
1 tomato, peeled and chopped
1/4 cup chopped fresh cilantro

Banana leaves or aluminum foil

Place the oregano, cumin, garlic, oil, and *Recado Rojo* or *achiote* paste in a blender or food processor and purée until smooth. Rub the marinade over the fish and marinate for 2 hours.

Sauté the shrimp, onion, and garlic in oil for a couple of minutes or until the shrimp is done. Add the tomato and cilantro and simmer for an additional 2 minutes.

Fill the fish with the shrimp mixture and place on the leaves or foil. Fold the leaves over the top and tie securely.

Place in a pan and bake, covered, in a 325 degree oven for 40 minutes.

Yield: 6 servings

Squid in Almond Sauce

Calamares Cancún

Squid has a very mild taste and shouldn't be overpowered by other ingredients. It can also become very rubbery and tough if overcooked, so sauté for approximately 4 minutes.

1 to 1 1/2 pounds squid, cleaned and cut into rings
4 tablespoons butter or margarine
1/2 cup dry white wine
1 tablespoon lime juice
3 tablespoons chopped fresh cilantro
1/2 cup almonds, toasted and finely chopped

Sauté the squid in the butter for a minute. Add the wine and lime juice and simmer for a few more minutes or until heated through.

Toss with the cilantro and almonds and serve.

Yield: 4 servings

Octopus in Its Ink

Pulpos en su Tinta

A very popular Yucatecan dish. Cooking an octopus in its ink can be very salty, so don't add any salt until you've tasted it.

2 large octopuses
2 tablespoons white vinegar
Water, to cover
3 tablespoons olive oil
1 large onion, chopped
2 fresh *chile dulce*, stems and seeds removed, chopped or substitute 1 small bell pepper
4 large cloves garlic, minced
2 large tomatoes, chopped
1 tablespoon chopped parsley
2 bay leaves
1/2 teaspoon ground cumin
1/2 teaspoon ground black pepper
1/2 teaspoon dried oregano, Mexican preferred

Remove the ink sacs from the octopuses and place them in the vinegar. The sacs will dissolve in the vinegar.

Cover the octopuses with water in a saucepan and simmer until they are done, from 2 to 3 hours. Remove the octopuses and discard the water. Cut the octopuses in small chunks.

Heat the oil until very hot. Sauté the onions, chile, and garlic. Add the tomatoes, parsley, bay leaves, cumin, black pepper, and oregano. Simmer for 5 minutes. Stir in the ink and vinegar mixture.

Bring to a boil, reduce the heat and simmer for 20 minutes. Add the octopus chunks and simmer for an additional 10 minutes.

Remove the stew from the heat and serve in bowls.

Yield: 4 to 6 servings

Vegetables, Fruit, Beans, and Rice

The warm tropical climate of the Yucatán is ideal for growing vegetables, as even a quick walk among the piles of beautiful vegetables in any market will confirm. Although food production is growing more commercialized every day in order to feed growing urban populations as well as millions of tourists, it is still based on small family operations. The typical rural family has a garden on the outskirts of their village where they raise some or all of the following vegetables: corn, pumpkins, tomatoes, beans, peppers, peas, tomatillos, carrots, potatoes, melons, radishes, onions, garlic, and squash.

Fruit trees including banana, mango, papaya, guava, coconut, mamey, tamarind, soursop, cherimoya, and a variety of citrus are generally planted around the home, as are herbs and spices. We have also seen many homes with cans or pots planted with various herbs or spices which were obviously intended for culinary use. In addition, it is not unusual to see a chile "tree" or two growing close to the house. Chiles are perennials and will grow into tree-sized plants in tropical climates.

City dwellers are forced to rely upon the local market for their vegetables. This is not really a hardship. The fruit and vegetable displays are attractive with precise little pyramids or huge piles of bright green and orange habanero chiles, alongside colorful displays of serrano, *poblano*, *xcatic*, and *dulce* chiles.

Next door might be a stack of huge avocados, each the size of a cantaloupe, while right across the way might be a stall with an array of bright orange, watermelon-sized papayas. Many different stalls display piles of citrus, mounds of onions and squash, stacks of carrots, cucumbers and lettuce, or crates full of potatoes. Brilliant red radishes are heaped up on a table next to a small mountain of dark red, ripe tomatoes, while peach-sized tomatillos overflow a giant wicker basket. And huge stalks of ripening bananas are on display everywhere. We think that it would be wonderful to be "forced" to buy our vegetables at markets like that!

Dried black beans, also called turtle beans, are one of the best known legumes from the Yucatán. They're very tasty and somewhat sweeter than the pinto beans most of us are used to eating as frijoles. They are also popular and, like corn, are served with every meal. They may be merely an ingredient in one dish, or served on the side as a vegetable, soup, or even as a dip or sauce, but they'll be there in some form.

Vegetables in the Yucatán are generally not served by themselves; most times they are combined with other vegetables or foods, along with herbs and spices, to create a totally different dish. We like this method of preparing and serving vegetables, which tends to make our servings of single vegetables rather bland. This chapter contains several recipes of this type including one of our favorites which combines squash, onion, chile, tomato, and cheese into a dish that we like so well that we sometimes eat it as an entree, rather than a vegetable.

Black Beans

Frijoles Negros

Tasty, sweet black beans, or turtle beans, are served throughout the Yucatán. In Mérida and Campeche they are served in a thin broth, almost like a soup, while in other areas we were offered a thicker mixture, more like refried beans. *Epazote* is always used to flavor the beans and because of its distinctive flavor, there really is no substitute. So, if you don't have any *epazote*, just omit it from the recipe.

1 pound black beans
Water, to cover
2 small onions, quartered
4 large cloves garlic
1 tablespoon dried *epazote*
1 fresh *habanero* chile, roasted, peeled, stem and seeds removed, chopped or substitute 2 fresh jalapeño or 3 serrano chiles

Cover the beans with water and soak overnight.

Bring to a boil, reduce the heat slightly and cook for an hour. Add the onions, garlic, *epazote*, and chiles. Simmer for an additional hour or until the beans are done.

Remove the onion, if possible, and mash the beans along with some of the water to a smooth consistency.

Yield: 6 servings

White Beans with Pork

Potage de Ibes

Although black beans are the most popular ones, there are a number of others available. In fact, we saw a wide variety in the markets. *Ibes*, or *frijoles blancos*, are a small white variety that is locally grown.

2 cups small white beans, such as navy beans
1/4 pound boneless pork, cut in 1 1/2-inch cubes
1 onion, chopped
2 cloves garlic, chopped
1 fresh *habanero* chile, stem and seeds removed, chopped or substitute 2 fresh jalapeño or 3 serrano chiles
1 tablespoon vegetable oil
2 small tomatoes, peeled and chopped
1 tablespoon *Recado Rojo* (page 21) or substitute *achiote* paste
1/4 teaspoon freshly ground black pepper

Cover the beans with water and soak overnight.

Bring the beans to a boil, reduce the heat and simmer for an hour. Add the pork, and continue to simmer until the beans are done, an additional hour.

Sauté the onion, garlic, and chiles in the oil until soft. Add the tomatoes, *Recado Rojo* or *achiote* paste, and black pepper, and simmer until the tomatoes break down to form a sauce.

Drain the beans and add to the sauce. Simmer until the mixture is heated throughout and the sauce has thickened.

Yield: 4 to 6 servings

Note: This recipe requires advance preparation.

Rice from Quintana Roo

Arroz Quintana Roo

This rice dish is not only tasty, but it also looks good and makes a nice accompaniment to almost any dish.

1 cup long-grain rice
1/2 onion, chopped
3 tablespoons butter or margarine
2 cups chicken broth
1 cup cooked, chopped *chaya* leaves, or substitute spinach or swiss chard
1 cup grated *queso asadero* or substitute Monterey Jack cheese

Sauté the rice and onion in the butter until the rice turns opaque and browns slightly.

Bring the broth to a boil, add the rice and onion mixture and bring back to a boil. Add the *chaya*, reduce the heat, and simmer for 25 minutes or until the rice is done.

Stir the rice to fluff it up. Place on a platter, top with the cheese and serve.

Yield: 4 to 6 servings

Yellow Rice

Arroz Amarillo

Annatto is used to color the rice, rather than add flavor, in this recipe. If you don't have any annatto, you can substitute a few threads of saffron that have been dissolved in water.

1 cup long-grain rice
1/2 purple onion, diced
3 serrano chiles, stems removed, sliced
3 cloves garlic, chopped
2 tablespoons butter or margarine
2 cups chicken broth
2 teaspoons ground annatto seeds
1 tomato, peeled and chopped
1/2 cup whole kernel corn
1/2 cup peas
1 teaspoon dried *epazote*
1 tablespoon chopped fresh cilantro

Sauté the rice, onion, chile, and garlic in butter until the rice turns opaque.

Bring the broth and annatto to a boil. Add the rice and bring back to a boil. Reduce the heat, stir in the tomato, corn, peas and *epazote* and cover. Simmer for 15 to 20 minutes or until the rice is done.

Garnish with the cilantro and serve.

Yield: 4 to 6 servings

Green Beans Chul

Chul de Frijol Verde

We took some liberties with this recipe to make it easier to prepare. Traditionally, the corn is mashed to make a thick sauce which is served with a salsa on the beans.

1 pound green beans, cut in 1 to 1 1/2-inch lengths
2 teaspoons *epazote*
2 tablespoons chopped onion
2 ears of corn
Water
3 tablespoons toasted pumpkin seeds, chopped

Simmer the beans in a little water along with the *epazote* and onion until the beans are tender. Drain them.

Cut the corn kernels from the ears and place in a pan along with any of the "corn milk" and a little water. Simmer until the corn is almost done.

Add the beans to the corn, mix well, and heat through.

Serve the beans in bowls garnished with the pumpkin seeds.

Yield: 4 servings

Zucchini with Cheese

Calabacitas con Queso

This simple and easy-to-prepare vegetable dish goes well with a wide variety of foods. *Añejo* is a sharp and tangy Mexican cheese. If not available, romano comes closest in flavor.

3 medium zucchini, cut in chunks or substitute yellow crookneck squash
1 small onion, diced
2 fresh jalapeño chiles, stems and seeds removed, chopped
1 tablespoon butter or margarine
2 tomatoes, chopped
1/2 cup shredded *queso añejo* cheese or substitute romano cheese

Steam the zucchini for 10 minutes or until done, but still slightly crunchy.

Sauté the onion and chiles in the butter until soft. Add the tomatoes and sauté for an additional 2 minutes.

Add the tomato mixture to the squash. Top with the cheese, cover and let sit for 5 minutes before serving.

Yield: 4 to 6 servings

Pickled Vegetables

Verduras en Escabeche

Serve these popular pickled vegetables as a vegetable side dish, salad, or even as a salsa.

1/2 small cauliflower, divided into flowerets
2 carrots, diced or julienned
1 small zucchini, diced or julienned
1 purple onion, sliced in thin rings
1 cup whole kernel corn
1/4 cup olive oil
2 tablespoons *Recado de Bistec* (page 21)
3/4 cup white or red wine vinegar
1 1/2 cups water

Cover the cauliflower, carrots, zucchini, onion, and corn with boiling water and let them sit off the heat for 15 minutes. Drain and wash with cold water.

Heat the oil and stir in the *Recado de Bistec*. Add the vegetables and sauté for a couple of minutes until cooked but still crispy.

Place the vegetables in a glass or ceramic bowl. Heat the vinegar and water to boiling and pour over the vegetables. Add more vinegar if needed to cover. Marinate for 12 hours.

Drain before serving.

Yield: 4 to 6 servings

Note: This recipe requires advance preparation.

Vegetables in Garlic Butter Sauce

Carrots and Chayote al Mojo de Ajo

The Restaurant Carabella in Progreso serves these vegetables as a side dish to *Pescado a la Plancha* (grilled fish). Adjust the amount of garlic to your taste.

2 tablespoons butter or margarine
1 tablespoons olive oil
5 cloves garlic, chopped
1/2 teaspoon ground red chile
1 tablespoon lime juice
2 carrots, peeled and cut julienne
1 small chayote, peeled and cut julienne or substitute 1 large zucchini

Melt the butter and olive oil in a pan. Add the garlic, chile, and lime juice and sauté the mixture for 2 to 3 minutes. Turn off the heat and let the mixture sit while the vegetables are cooking.

Steam the vegetables until soft but still slightly crisp. Drain.

Remove the garlic cloves and toss the vegetables in the garlic butter until coated and serve.

Yield: 4 to 6 servings

Corn and Cabbage with *Epazote*

Esquites

Corn is the most popular vegetable in the Yucatán, but this recipe, which combines corn with cabbage, is rather an unusual combination. We enjoyed this interesting dish several times in Campeche.

1/2 cup chopped onions
1 clove garlic, minced
1 tablespoon vegetable oil
2 cups shredded cabbage
2 cups whole kernel corn
1 teaspoon dried *epazote*
Chopped fresh cilantro for garnish

Sauté the onions and garlic in the oil. Add the cabbage and sauté until it begins to soften. Add the remaining ingredients and cook until the vegetables are done.

Garnish with the cilantro and serve.

Yield: 4 to 6 servings

Chayote Pudding

Budín de Chayote

Making puddings out of vegetables is very popular in the Yucatán. Corn, zucchini, pumpkin, and even pinto beans are a few of the vegetables that are used. *Budíns* are sometimes served as a light entrée or even as a dessert, since they are quite sweet.

4 small *chayotes*
Water, to cover
4 eggs
1 1/2 tablespoons butter or margarine
4 tablespoons sugar
1 teaspoon vanilla
1 teaspoon ground cinnamon

Cover the whole *chayotes* with water, bring to a boil, reduce the heat and simmer until the squash are tender, about 30 to 40 minutes. Remove and discard water. Peel and coarsely chop.

Place all of the ingredients in a blender or food processor and purée until smooth. Pour the mixture into an oiled round mold.

Bake in a 325 degree oven for 30 to 35 minutes or until the pudding is firm.

Carefully unmold and serve.

Yield: 4 to 6 servings

Desserts and Drinks

Although a wide variety of sweets including candy, ice cream, and pastries are consumed in the Yucatán, desserts are often not even listed on restaurant menus. Tourist restaurants generally offer full selections, but local eateries may offer only a flan or maybe a sweet fruit dish such as fried plantains. This is because the local custom is to go to a specialty store, like an ice cream or pastry shop, for dessert. We've grown to enjoy this custom, and after finishing a meal, we often find ourselves wandering over to the closest pastry shop.

Pastries in Mexico are usually excellent, and pastry shops can be found in nearly all decent-sized towns. The bigger the town, the bigger the selection. Shops in small towns may offer only a dozen different pastries, while the larger shops in Mérida offer more than a hundred. If you're a lover of pastry, cakes, and breads, we've found a bit of heaven on earth for you, and its name is El Sol.

Located in Mérida on Calle 56 (56th Street) close to the Post Office, El Sol offers an enormous selection. The assortment is so vast that it's difficult to make decisions, especially since there is very little that looks familiar. For instance, what would a pastry shaped like a turtle taste like, and what sort of filling could possibly be inside the one that looks like an iguana? Loaves of bread and rolls and layered cakes are certainly recognizable, but when you're dealing with pastries, prepare to be bewildered and surprised.

For starters, there are no donuts or danish pastries. If you do see something that looks familiar, remember that looks can be deceiving. We remember a shop in Campeche, where we picked out a pastry that we were sure was filled with fruit of some sort, only to find a cold hot dog inside! But that's half the fun, to bite into something and be totally surprised. Over the years we have sampled dozens and possibly hundreds of different baked treats, and while there were a few that we didn't care for, there are many that we have grown to love and simply can't resist. Generally speaking, the pastries are less sweet than U.S. equivalents, although when the Mexicans decide to make something sweet, they really make it sweet!

Our first visit to the El Sol was one we won't forget. It was around six one evening, and the place was mobbed; it could hardly have been more crowded had they been handing it out for free. People on their way home from work filled the shop from wall to wall, all carrying trays, bumping into anyone in their way and squeezing their tongs between other shoppers in order to pile up pastries and cookies and pieces of cake like this was the last chance they'd ever get. We were moving slowly, trying to make sense of the vast selection in the midst of the chaos around us, and as a result, we got bumped into and jostled continuously. Nobody was picking on us or being particularly rude, it was simply a question of too many people trying to rush through too small a space. We finally made it out of the shop alive with pastry bag clutched firmly in hand, dazzled by the selection, and in a daze from the crowd. We laugh a lot over that crazy memory!

Because of the heat, iced drinks are very popular, especially iced fruit drinks. Some of the most brightly colored shops in the cities are those that sell the fruit drinks. Usually no more than a long counter in front of a wall of fruit, these shops are also some of the busiest. The delicious, puréed fruit drinks that they sell are made to order from a wide variety of fresh fruit, either alone or in imaginative combinations. We drink a lot of these icy treats when we travel in the Yucatán, and also prepare them quite often at home during the summer.

Flan

Queso Napolitano

Spanish in origin, flans are very popular throughout Mexico. This regional recipe produces a flan that is firmer than most, almost like cheesecake.

2/3 cup sugar
1/4 cup water
1 14-ounce can condensed milk
1 12-ounce can evaporated milk
6 eggs
1 tablespoon vanilla
8 ounces Philadelphia cream cheese
Flan pan

Preheat oven to 350 degrees.

Combine the sugar and water in a heavy saucepan and while heating, stir several times to dissolve the sugar. Bring to a boil, reduce the heat to medium, and simmer while swirling the pan until the sugar turns golden and is caramelized. Immediately pour into the flan mold and tilt so that it covers the bottom of the pan.

Combine the remaining ingredients and beat until smooth. Pour into the mold. Cover the mold with foil.

Place the mold in a pan of water that reaches to within an inch of the top. Put in the center of the oven and bake for 40 to 50 minutes or until a knife inserted in the center comes out clean.

Cool completely before unmolding.

Yield: 12 servings

Heavenly Cake

Torta del Cielo

This special cake is reserved for weddings, birthdays, and other specific occasions in the Yucatán. There are many versions, including some that use only ground almonds and no flour at all.

8 ounces blanched raw almonds
1/2 cup all-purpose flour
1 teaspoon baking powder
10 eggs, separated
1 1/4 cups sugar
1 tablespoon rum
1/4 teaspoon cream of tartar
Pinch of salt
Confectioners' sugar
1/4 cup chopped toasted almonds

Preheat oven to 350 degrees.

Line the bottom of a 10-inch springform pan with wax paper and oil the paper.

Grind the almonds until very fine. Sift with the flour and baking powder.

Beat the egg yolks and gradually add the sugar until light, thick and creamy. Beat in the flour mixture and then the rum.

Beat egg whites with the cream of tartar and salt until they form firm peaks. Fold 1/3 of the egg whites into the egg and flour mixture. Fold this mixture into the remaining whites only until the last of the whites disappear. Do not overmix.

Pour the batter into the springform pan and bake for 40 minutes or until the top is browned and starts to pull away from the sides. Allow to cool completely before removing from the pan.

Decorate with a dusting of confectioners' sugar and coarsely chopped almonds.

Yield: 10 servings

Seashells

Conchas

Pan dulce, or sweet breads, are probably the most common and popular bakery item in all of Mexico. They can be found in a number of shapes and even a variety of colors. This version is called conchas because the pattern the sugar topping forms as the dough rises makes it look like a seashell. In Mexico they have a special metal ring tool that when pressed on top of the roll makes the pattern, but a knife will work equally as well.

Dough

1 package dry yeast
1 cup warm water
1/2 teaspoon salt
1 cup sugar, divided
1 cup milk
1 egg, beaten
1/4 cup butter or margarine, melted
4 cups sifted all-purpose flour

Topping

1/2 cup butter or margarine
1 cup sugar
1 egg yolk
1 teaspoon cinnamon (optional)
1/2 cup all-purpose flour

Dissolve the yeast in the water. Add the salt and 1/2 cup sugar. Let sit for 15 minutes.

Heat the milk until a film forms on top. Remove and cool to room temperature. Add to the yeast mixture along with the remaining sugar, egg, and butter.

Add the flour to the liquid, 1 cup at a time, until you cannot stir in any more. Turn onto a floured board and knead for 8 to 10 minutes or until dough is smooth and elastic. Place the dough in a greased bowl, cover with a cloth and let rise until double in size, about 1 1/2 to 2 hours.

To make the topping, cream the butter and sugar. Add the egg yolk and cinnamon. Add the flour and mix well; you may have to use your hands as the mixture will be crumbly. Divide into 12 flattened pancakes.

Divide the dough into 12 equal portions and form into round flattened buns. Place a topping pancake on each bun, press into the dough slightly, and using a knife cut a crisscross pattern through the topping.

Place the rolls on a greased baking dish and allow to rise for an additional hour or until again doubled.

Bake in a 400 degree oven for 15 to 20 minutes or until very lightly browned. Do not overbake as they will become hard.

Yield: 12 conchas

Kings' Cave

Rocas de Reyes

Rocas de Reyes is served on All Kings' Day, January 6th, that celebrates the three kings of the nativity. Traditionally, the cake is baked with a small doll in the center and whoever gets the piece with the doll must host a party on Candlemas Day. Other traditions say the person who gets the doll will have good luck, or if it is a girl, she will be married within the year.

Cake

1 package dry yeast
1/2 cup lukewarm water
3 to 4 cups sifted all-purpose flour, divided
1/4 pound unsalted butter, melted
1/4 cup sugar
4 egg yolks, beaten
2 eggs, beaten
1 cup condensed milk
2 teaspoons grated lemon rind
1/2 teaspoon salt
1 to 2 cups candied fruit, chopped

Topping

3 tablespoons heavy cream
1 cup sifted confectioners' sugar
Candied fruit, cut in strips

Combine the yeast with the water and add 1/2 cup of the flour. Mix well and gather into a ball. Allow the mixture to rise for 30 minutes or until doubled in size.

Mix the butter, sugar, eggs, milk, lemon rind, and salt together.

Gradually add the yeast mixture and candied fruits. Add the remaining flour a little at a time. Turn the dough onto a floured board and knead for 10 minutes or until smooth and elastic. Place in a greased bowl and let rise for 2 hours or until doubled in size.

Punch the dough down and let sit for 5 minutes. Shape the dough into a ring and place on a greased baking sheet. Allow to rise for 1 to 2 hours or until double in size.

Bake at 350 degrees for 25 to 30 minutes or until browned. Remove and cool slightly.

Combine the cream and sugar and mix to form a thick icing. Spread over the cooled ring and allow to drip down the sides. Garnish with the candied fruit.

Yield: 12 servings

Orange Cake

Pastel de Naranja

Orange-flavored cakes and muffins were some of our favorites. The bitter oranges used in the Yucatán will give a different flavor, but orange juice, zest and lime juice are a good substitute.

Cake

1 1/4 cup all-purpose flour
1 teaspoon double-acting baking powder
1 teaspoon baking soda
1/2 teaspoon salt
1/2 cup butter or margarine, softened
1 1/2 cups sugar
4 eggs, separated
2 teaspoons grated orange zest
1 teaspoon almond extract
1 cup blanched toasted almonds, coarsely ground
1 cup orange juice

Filling

3 tablespoons cornstarch
2 cups orange juice
1/4 cup lime juice
1/2 teaspoon salt
1 cup sugar
2 egg yolks, beaten
4 tablespoons melted butter or margarine
1 teaspoon orange extract

Glaze

1/4 cup sugar
1/2 cup orange juice
2 tablespoons butter or margarine

Preheat the oven to 350 degrees.

Sift the dry cake ingredients except the ground almonds together.

Cream the butter and sugar together until fluffy. Lightly beat the egg yolks. Add to the butter mixture along with the orange zest and almond extract. Stir in the coarsely ground almonds.

Alternate adding the flour mixture and orange juice to the butter, beginning and ending with the dry ingredients.

Beat the egg whites until stiff but not dry and gently fold into the cake batter.

Spoon the batter into three 8-inch greased cake pans. Bake for 25 to 30 minutes or until the cakes are done. Cool cakes completely.

To make the filling, stir the cornstarch into the orange juice. Add the lime juice, salt, and sugar. Beat the egg yolks and add them, along with the butter, to the filling. Quickly bring the mixture to a boil, reduce the heat and simmer for 5 minutes. Remove from the heat, cool, and stir in the orange extract. Refrigerate to chill.

To assemble, spread the chilled filling between the cake layers. Combine and heat the glaze ingredients and pour over the layered cake.

Allow the cake to cool and the glaze to set before serving.

Yield: 10 servings

Candied Sweet Papaya

Dulce de Papaya

The slight tartness of the *crema agria* complements the sweetness of this dessert.

1/4 cup sugar
1/4 cup water
2 tablespoons honey
1 pound papaya, cut into 1-inch cubes
1 tablespoon fresh lime juice
***Crema Agria* (see the following recipe)**

Combine the sugar and water in a heavy pan and while heating, stir to dissolve the sugar. Add the honey and simmer over a low heat until the syrup starts to thicken, about 10 minutes. Be careful that the syrup does not begin to change color or caramelize.

Add the papaya and lime juice and mix to coat. Simmer the fruit for 20 minutes or until the liquid is reduced by half.

Chill well and serve with *Crema Agria* on the side.

Yield: 4 servings

Cream Sauce

Crema Agria

This is the Mexican version of the French *crème fraîche*.

2 cups heavy cream, room temperature
1/4 cup buttermilk, room temperature

Combine the cream and buttermilk in a bowl and place plastic wrap on the surface of the mixture. Let stand in warm area until mixture thickens, about 18 hours. Stir thoroughly and refrigerate until ready to use. It will keep for a couple of weeks.

Yield: 2 cups

Note: This recipe requires advance preparation.

Sweet Rice Enchiladas

Postre de Leche

This is a Yucatecan variation of the very popular rice pudding that is served all over Mexico. Traditionally corn tortillas are used, but we have substituted flour tortillas which make a lighter dessert.

2 cups cooked rice
1 cup condensed milk
1/2 cup evaporated milk
1/4 cup sugar
1 teaspoon cinnamon
3 tablespoons raisins, soaked in hot water and drained
6 small flour tortillas
Vegetable oil
1/2 teaspoon ground cinnamon
1/2 cup sugar

Combine the rice, milk, sugar, and cinnamon and simmer over a low heat until most of the moisture has been absorbed. Stir in the raisins.

Place a portion of the rice on a tortilla, roll, secure with a toothpick. Fry in 1/2 inch of oil until lightly browned. Remove and drain.

Arrange on a serving platter and lightly dust with cinnamon and sugar combined.

Yield: 6 servings

Fried Plantains Caribbean Style

Plantanos Fritos Caribeños

Honey has been a popular sweetener in the Yucatán since pre-Hispanic times. The Maya cultivated bees for their honey and to this day hives are found all over the peninsula.

1/4 cup butter or margarine
1/4 teaspoon cinnamon
4 medium plantains, ripe but still firm, peeled and sliced lengthwise or substitute bananas
1/4 cup honey
1/2 cup *Crema Agria* (page 99)

Melt the butter in a saucepan and add the cinnamon. Place the plantains in the butter mixture and sauté for a couple of minutes on each side until golden.

Place the plantains on a serving platter, spoon a little of the honey over each, and top with a dollop of *Crema Agria.*

Yield: 4 to 6 servings

Pineapple Turnovers

Empanadas Con Piña

Empanadas, a Mexican or Spanish version of a turnover, can be found stuffed with a wide variety of fillings, including meats, fruits, and nuts. These *piña* or pineapple *empanadas* include the tropical fruits that are popular in the Yucatán.

Dough

2 cups flour, sifted
2 tablespoons sugar
2 teaspoons baking powder
3/4 cup cold butter or margarine, cut in small pieces
1 egg separated
1/4 cup ice water

Filling

1/2 cup pineapple juice, fresh or canned
2 tablespoons cornstarch
3 tablespoons sugar
2 cups diced fresh pineapple or substitute canned, unsweetened, drained pineapple
1/2 cup sliced almonds or chopped walnuts
1/2 cup unsweetened shredded coconut, fresh or dried
1/4 cup raisins

Sift together all the dry ingredients. Cut the butter into the mixture using a pastry blender or two forks until the flour resembles fine crumbs.

Beat the egg yolk and water together. Gradually add just enough to the dry ingredients until they just hold together. Chill for an hour.

Turn the dough onto a floured board, roll out to 1/8 inch thick and cut into 4-inch circles.

Combine the pineapple juice and cornstarch in a saucepan and heat. Add the sugar and stir to dissolve. Add the pineapple and bring to a boil, stirring constantly. Reduce the heat and simmer until the sauce has thickened.

Remove from the heat, stir in the remaining ingredients, and allow to cool before filling the empanadas.

Place approximately 1 tablespoon filling on half of each circle and fold over. Moisten the edges with water and crimp with a fork to seal.

Place on an ungreased baking pan. Lightly beat the egg white and brush the tops of the empanadas.

Bake in a 400 degree oven for 15 minutes or until lightly browned.

Yield: 15 to 18 empanadas; 2 1/2 to 3 cups sauce

Marzipan

Melindres de Yepes

We found these colorful candies throughout the Yucatán in a wide variety of shapes and colors. These popular sweets are most often shaped and colored like vegetables and fruits, from bananas to chile peppers.

1 pound raw almonds
3 cups powdered sugar
3 egg whites

Pour boiling water over the almonds and let them stand for a couple of minutes. Remove the skins. Allow to dry completely. Grind in a food processor or blender until very fine (you may have to grind them a couple of times).

Add the sugar and continue to blend until a thick paste forms.

Whip the egg whites until they are stiff and gradually add the almond paste. Mix well.

Pinch off a couple of tablespoons, mix in food coloring very thoroughly and shape into desired shapes. Repeat.

Yield: 2 trips to the dentist

Ground Rice Drink

Agua de Horchata

The Spaniards, who were familiar with drinks made from steeped nuts and grains, brought the idea for this drink to the New World. In the Yucatán, however, rice was used as the base, and the drink became and has remained extremely popular.

2 cups long-grain rice
6 cups water
2 teaspoons ground cinnamon
Sugar

Place the rice in a spice or coffee grinder and process as fine as possible. Cover with the water and soak for 3 hours.

Add the cinnamon and simmer for 10 minutes.

Cool and strain through cheesecloth, squeezing the rice to extract all the liquid.

Dilute with enough water to make 4 cups, add sugar to taste, and serve.

Yield: 1 quart or 6 to 8 servings

Variation
Dilute with milk for a creamier drink.

Spiced Coffee

Cafe de Olla

Popular throughout Mexico, this spiced coffee is made in clay pots called *ollas*.

1 quart water
1 4-inch stick cinnamon
4 whole cloves
2 tablespoons brown sugar
6 tablespoons freshly ground coffee

Bring the water to a boil, add the cinnamon and cloves, and infuse for a couple minutes. Add the sugar and stir until it dissolves. Stir in the coffee, and while stirring constantly, bring back to a boil. Remove from the heat and let sit for 3 minutes.

Strain into small cups and serve with cream or milk.

Yield: 6 to 8 servings

Fresh Fruit Drinks

Agua Fresca

Anyone who has traveled in Mexico has seen these refreshing fruit drinks sold on street corners. We've used melon in this recipe, but almost any fruit can be used. Just be sure to adjust the amount of sugar, which will depend on the sweetness of the fruit.

3 cups cubed fresh melon (cantaloupe, honeydew, or watermelon)
4 tablespoons sugar
3 tablespoons lime juice, fresh preferred
1 quart water
Melon slices for garnish

Combine the fruit, sugar, and lime juice in a blender and purée until smooth. Add the purée to the water and mix.

Garnish each glass with a melon slice before serving.

Yield: 1 quart

Appendix

Cooking Tips and Techniques

Grinding Annatto. Since it is a very hard seed, use a spice or coffee grinder, sift the results, and regrind. Repeat as often as necessary to produce a fine powder.

Banana Leaves. Use as a tamale wrap, with poultry, meats, and fish. Wash all leaves before using. To thaw or soften, pass over a gas flame or hold over an electric burner for several seconds until leaves begin to turn light green and are softened. Remove the center ribs from the leaves and save them for tying.

Bitter Oranges. This rough-skinned Yucatecan fruit tastes more like a grapefruit with a hint of orange than an orange. A suitable substitute can be made using the following recipe. I find that using fresh squeezed juices produces the best results.

Bitter Orange Juice

1/2 cup grapefruit juice
1/4 cup orange juice
3 tablespoons lime juice

Mix all of the ingredients in a glass bowl and let stand at room temperature for 2 hours. Use within 24 hours.

Yield: 3/4 cup

Roasting Vegetables. Preheat a dry skillet or *comal* (tortilla griddle) until very hot. Place the unpeeled vegetables on the skillet and roast for 10 to 15 minutes, turning frequently. If you have a stovetop grill, place over the burner and roast the vegetables over the flame until the skins are blackened, about 5 minutes. You can also roast them under a broiler. After roasting, remove the skins and chop. If you are roasting garlic heads, use an oven.

Tamales. To wrap, use either a softened banana leaf (see above) or corn husks that have been soaked in water until soft. Lay the tamale wrapper on a flat surface. Place about 2 tablespoons *masa* in the center, and pat or spread the dough thinly and evenly. Place the filling down the center of the *masa* and fold the wrapper around the *masa* and filling, folding the *masa* over the filling in the process. Fold the wrapper as tightly as possible, being careful not to squeeze the tamale, and fold under the ends. Tie the tamale around the center with string or the reserved rib from the banana leaves.

Toasting Chiles. Place the chiles on a cookie sheet in a 250 degree oven and toast for 5 minutes, being careful not to let them burn.

Toasting Seeds or Nuts. Heat a griddle or *comal* until very hot. Toast the seeds or nuts until they start to brown and begin to "pop." Do not let them burn. Cool completely before grinding, or they will clump up in the grinder.

Glossary of Foods

Achiote (ah-chee-OH-tay). Seasoning paste made of ground annatto seeds, herbs, and bitter orange juice.

Adobo (ah-DOH-bo). A thick cooking sauce composed of tomatoes, vinegar, and spices.

Albóndigas (al-BON-dee gahs). Meatballs.

Ancho Chile (AHN-cho). The dried form of the poblano chile. It is the most widely used dried chile in Mexico.

Annatto (ah-NAH-toh). The small, red-orange seed of the annatto tree (Bixa orellana) that is used for seasoning and coloring.

Antojito (ahn-to-HEE-toe). Literally, "little whim," an appetizer usually made from corn masa.

Arroz (ah-ROHS). Rice

Banana Leaves (Hoja de Platano). Available in Latin and Asian markets, frozen. Used extensively in the Yucatán for wrapping tamales and for cooking foods in the pibil style. The leaves impart a distinctive taste to foods.

Bitter Orange. Also goes by the name sour orange, Seville orange, and *naranja agria* (sour orange). A rough-skinned Yucatecan citrus fruit that tastes more like a grapefruit with an orange chaser.

Budín (boo-DEEN). A sweet pudding made from vegetables.

Calamari (ca-la-MAR-ee). Squid.

Camarones (ka-ma-ROH-nays). Shrimp.

Cazón (ka-ZOHN). Dogfish shark.

Ceviche (sah-VEE-chee). Raw seafood combined with citrus juice, which "cooks" the fish by combining with its protein and turning it opaque.

Chayote (cha-YO-tey). Called a mirliton in the southern U.S., it's a pear-shaped member of the squash family primarily grown in Mexico.

Chile. The plant or pod of the genus Capsicum.

Chile de árbol (ARE-bol). A thin, hot dried red chile from Mexico. Substitute dried red New Mexican chiles or Chiltepins.

Chile Dulce (DUL-say). Large, multilobed, bright green chile resembling an *habanero* but with no heat.

***Chipotle* Chile** (chee-POHT-lay). A smoked and dried jalapeño chile.

Cilantro (see-LAN-tro). An annual herb (Coriandrum sativum) with seeds (which are known as coriander), also called Chinese parsley. Substitute Italian parsley.

Cochinita Pibil (co-cha-NEE-ta pee-BEEL). Pork marinated with achiote paste, wrapped in banana leaves, and baked in a stone-lined pit.

Cumin. An annual herb (Cuminum cyminum) with seeds that have a distinctive odor.

Epazote (eh-pah-SOH-tay). Pungent, bitter, almost mint-like perennial herb (Chenopodium ambrosiodes). Used to season beans and sauces. Also goes by the name wormseed. There is no substitute—omit it if you don't have it.

Escabeche (es-kah-BEH-chay). Vegetables marinated or pickled in vinegar with seasonings.

Garnacha (gar-NAY-cha). Thick corn tortilla, stuffed with beans and topped with pork or chicken, onions, and avocados.

***Habanero* chile** (ah-ba-NARE-row). Literally, "from Havana"; a small orange or red chile from the Yucatán; strong, distinctive flavor and the hottest in the world. Substitute jalapeños or serranos.

Jalapeño chile (hal-la-PEH-nyo). A small, hot, fat chile; it is pickled, stuffed, or used fresh. Substitute serrano chiles.

Jícama (HEE-ka-mah). A white tuber (Pachyrhizus erosus) used in salads; it tastes like a cross between an apple, potato, and water chestnut.

Limas Agrias (LEE-mahs AH-gree-ahs). Similar to Key limes, smaller, darker green, and tarter than Persian limes common in this country.

Masa (MAH-sa). Dough made from ground dried corn and water.

Masa Harina (MAH-sa ha-REE-na). Corn flour.

Mexican Oregano. A shrub (Lippia graveolens) from Mexico with a different and stronger flavor than European oregano (Origanum vulgare).

Nopal/Nopalito (no-PAHL/no-pah-LEE-toh). The pad of the prickly pear cactus, spines removed. Available fresh or canned. Rinse well to remove the sticky substance before using.

Pan de Cazón (payn day ka-ZOHN). Three layers of corn tortillas, black beans, and shark meat, topped with a tomato sauce.

Panuchos (pa-NEW-chos). Tortillas stuffed with black beans and topped with shredded turkey or chicken.

Papadzules (papa-DULE-say). Enchiladas stuffed with hard-boiled eggs, pepitas, and topped with tomato sauce.

***Pasilla* chile** (pah-SEE-yah). Literally, "little raisin," alluding to the aroma and dark brown color of the long, thin, wrinkled, mild Mexican chile.

Pavo (PAA-vo). Turkey.

Pepita (pah-PEE-tah). Roasted pumpkin seeds.

Pibil (pe-BEEL). Pit-baked

Picadillo (pee-ka-DEE-yo). Shredded beef, spices, and other ingredients usually used as a stuffing.

Pipián (pe-PEYAHN). A sauce containing spices and ground nuts or seeds.

***Poblano* chile** (po-BLAN-o). Literally, "pepper of the people," dark-green, fat, mild chile commonly used throughout Mexico. The dried form is called ancho.

Queso (KAY-so). Cheese.
añejo—dry, salty cheese, use grated as garnish, substitute romano
asadero—mild, soft cheese, used melted, substitute Monterey Jack, mozzarella, or provolone

chihuahua—mild, nutty cheese, substitute Monterey Jack or cheddar

Recado (ra-CA-do). Seasoning paste from the Yucatán.

Relleno (ray-YA-no). Stuffed.

Salbutes (sal-BOO-tays). Fried tortillas, covered with shredded turkey, pickled onion, and additional toppings.

Salpicón (sal-pee-CON). A Mexican shredded salad of meat or radishes. Anything with ingredients in little pieces.

Salsa. Literally, "sauce," but usually used to describe uncooked sauces (salsa cruda).

Serrano chile (say-RAN-o). A small hot Mexican chile. Substitute jalapeños.

Tamale. Any filling enclosed in *masa*, wrapped in husks, and steamed.

Tomatillo (toe-ma-TEE-o). A small green tomato with papery husk (*Physalis ixocarpa*).

Xcatic **chile** (sch-KA-tik). Pale yellow or green chile, 5 to 7 inches long. Substitute banana or *güero* chiles.

Yerba Buena (yur-ba BWEY-na). Spearmint.

Mail-Order Sources

Cookbooks and Publications

Chile Pepper Magazine
P.O. Box 4278
Albuquerque, NM 87196
(800) 359-1483

Jessica's Biscuit
P.O. Box 301
Newtonville, MA 02160
(800) 878-4264

Out West Publishing
P.O. Box 4278
Albuquerque, NM 87196
(800) 359-1483

Food and Mexican Ingredients

Colorado Spice Company
5030 Nome St.
Denver, CO 80239
(303) 373-9215

Coyote Cafe
1364 Rufina Circle #1
Santa Fe, NM 87501
(505) 982-2454

Don Alfonso Foods
P.O. Box 201988
Austin, TX 78720
(800) 456-6100

Old Southwest Trading Company
P.O. Box 7545
Albuquerque, NM 87194
(505) 836-0168

Pendery's Spices
304 Belknap
Fort Worth, TX 76102
(800) 533-1870

Stonewall Chili Pepper Co.
Highway 290, Box 241
Stonewall, TX
(800) 232-2995

Bibliography

Fodor's 92 Cancún, Cozumel, Yucatán Peninsula, New York: Fodor's Travel Publications, 1991.

Frommer's Yucatán, New York: Prentice Hall, 1993.

Bayless, Rick, and Deann Groen Bayless, *Authentic Mexican, Regional Cooking from the Heart of Mexico*, New York: William Morrow, 1987.

Cadwallader, Sharon, *Savoring Mexico*, San Francisco: Chronicle Books, 1980.

Carlson, Lorraine, *The TraveLeer Guide to Yucatán and Guatemala: The World of the Maya*, Chicago: Upland Press, 1980.

Childress, Marjorie, and Clyde Childress, *Adventures in Mexican Cooking*, San Francisco: Ortho Books, 1978.

DeWitt, Dave, and Nancy Gerlach, *The Whole Chile Pepper Book*, Boston: Little Brown and Company, 1990.

Elverson, Virginia, *Gulf Coast Cooking*, Texas: Shearer Publishing, 1991.

Holt, Paula, and Helene Juarez, *Authentic Mexican Cooking*, New York: Simon and Schuster, 1984.

Kennedy, Diana, *The Art of Mexican Cooking*, New York: Bantam Books, 1989.

The Cuisines of Mexico, New York: Harper and Row, 1989.

Martinez, Zarela, *Food from My Heart*, New York: Macmillan, 1992.

Mallan, Chicki, *Yucatán Handbook*, 3rd ed., Chico, CA: Moon Publications, 1990.

Mulvey, Ruth Watt, *Good Food from Mexico*, New York: M. Barrows, 1950.

Ortiz, Elisabeth, *The Complete Book of Mexican Cooking*, New York: Ballantine Books, 1967.

Palazuelos, Susanna, *Mexico the Beautiful Cookbook: Authentic Recipes from the Regions of Mexico*, San Francisco: Collins, 1991.

Quintana, Patricia, *The Taste of Mexico*, New York: Stewart, Tambori and Chang, 1986.

Ringland, Eleanor, and Lucy Ringland Winston, *Fiestas Mexicanas: Menus and Recipes*, San Antonio, TX: Naylor, 1967.

Simon, Kate, *Mexico, Places and Pleasures*, 3rd ed., New York: Thomas Y. Crowell, 1979.

Stevens, John L., *Incidents of Travel in Central America, Chiapas, and Yucatán*, Reprint, New York: Dover, 1969.

Wright, Ronald, *Time Among the Maya*, New York: Weidenfeld and Nicholson, 1989.

Index

D

E

F

G

H

I

J

K

L

Q

R

S

T

U

V

W

X

Y

Z